The *Sabi*

Book One: by Diane Brown

New Generation Publishing

"For Carl"

Thanks and Appreciation

To my soul friend, Thandiwe, you are an amazing woman and the world is better for it. You affirm my voice and you take me, just as I am. Thank you;

To my gifted and caring daughter, in saying "you look so different when you write, so beautiful mom," affirmed this undertaking. Thanks for your spirit and the ability to see beauty around you;

To my son, blessed with wisdom who forgives my very many flaws and asks me to read one more page. Thanks for seeing the tracks etched on my face;

To a fine young man, my nephew Tremaine, for giving me a break when it counted. Thanks for your kind heart and your shoulder;

To my dear mother who told me that I could do anything. I see the tracks etched on your face and knees mom. Thanks for the untold sacrifices;

To my dad who lived possibilities rather than just spoke of them. Thanks for the phone calls and for the last dance on my birthday, though you were frail. I heard you on this day when you whispered "I am proud of you";

To Allen who wanted to know more and made me feel that what I had to say, mattered;

To my sister, who makes it possible for me to sleep with both eyes closed when I am with her;

To Mandla, Richard, Lentswe, Tanya, Mpho, Josie, Busisiwe, Alicia, Mavuso, Angy, Maxwell, the Kunutu's and the Keet's who crossed my path at the right time and who saved me in ways that they are yet to know;

To Ezra who gets me, thanks for your friendship and calming influence; and

To Yves who in the times when it really mattered, never doubted me. Merci de croire en cette endeavour aussi, le vin rouge, la patience et conversations.

And lastly to my dear friend Gerald for giving me the hours of conversation and friendship every day for a year when I needed it most, and for inspiring the title of this book. I sabi, you sabi!

1

Foreword

Learn from yesterday, live for today,
hope for tomorrow.
The important thing is to not stop questioning.
Albert Einstein

South Africa, a rainbow nation and home to the iconic Nelson Mandela, who is celebrated across the world. This country is indeed a miracle. I would boldly say that South Africans love South Africa. Our love for this country grows every time we leave its shores, for it is when we leave that we realise what it is we have actually left behind, and then we begin to long and pine for it. When you witness packed stadiums for soccer, rugby, cricket, music concerts and rallies, know that that is an expression of the love that South Africans have for this country. When you witness busy talk shows with divergent opinions, cares and concerns, this is an expression of the love South Africans have for their country.

We have many achievements and much that we are proud of. We have produced ten Nobel Prize winners, in categories ranging through Chemistry, Literature, Peace, and Medicine. The Dragon became the first commercially built and operated spacecraft to be recovered successfully from orbit, thanks to South African born Elon Musk, and later the first to be attached to the International Space Station. Musk was also cofounder of PayPal, the e-commerce business allowing payment and transfers through the internet. We have set the standards in heart transplants, and even JRR Tolkien, the creator of the *Lord of the Rings*, was born in this country.

This country is blessed with rich mineral resources, land, sunny skies and heritage sites worth visiting and admiring. It has amazing scenery and weather, and is one of the greatest places in the world for any tourist to visit. I have travelled all over the world and each time I look forward to returning home because this is my country and it indeed is beautiful, and has so much potential and many unearthed possibilities.

We also have the good fortune of naming as citizens Steve Biko, Nelson Mandela, Desmond Tutu, Charlize Theron, Oliver Reginald Tambo, Dennis Brutus, Chad le Clos, Kumi Naidoo, Mrs Ples, Mark Shuttleworth and Gavin Hood.

The Oprah Winfrey Leadership Academy for Girls graces South Africa, and I am pleased that Oprah absorbed the start-up problems of establishing this school, because heaven knows that this country needs a place where girls can learn in an environment that honours who they are. I look forward to seeing the women leaders who will emerge from this place. I celebrate the attention to detail she personally put into the architecture, the cutlery and the linen, because that is what girls in this country need to feel – that they are special and that they are worth the effort, the time and the outward expression of love and care that she demonstrated in this process.

We have hosted international summits on Sustainable Development, Climate Change and Conservation and we host the Pan-African Parliament in Johannesburg. We are a well organised country with impressive road and hotel infrastructure. We have the Gautrain as a basis for developing a robust, timeous and efficient transport system and which will also go a long way in reducing the use of cars on our roads so that we can reduce our individual and national carbon footprint.

And we are a sports loving nation. We have successfully hosted the Rugby World Cup, the FIFA Soccer World Cup, the Cricket World Cup and the Africa Cup of Nations. We are only the second country to win the Rugby World Cup twice. We hold the top spots in the world for top Test Cricket Team, top bowler, top batsman and top all rounder.

Then there are the unsung heroes, the ones that do not get the accolades but whose integrity and sacrifice build this country one block at a time. Those who died and gave up their freedoms so that we can be free. Those ordinary women and men who work hard each day to make sure that the next generation can have better opportunities than they had. Those officials in government who choose to have integrity, work hard and go the extra mile to make a difference. Those boys and girls who still believe that there is something that they can learn from those who have hindsight on their side. That single mother who sacrifices much so her children can grow up to be outliers some day. That civil society worker that works tirelessly to let the voice of the voiceless be heard. That activist, although a lone voice sometimes, who chooses to speak out no matter what the cost. That father who chooses to take care of his children without having to be taken to court. That policeman who chooses to protect and serve. That nurse who is driven to care for the aged and the sick. That young man and woman who embrace the accents of all South Africans and choose not to label people because of the way they speak. That young man who chooses not to disrespect and rape the girl whose drink has been laced. That young girl who reports violence against her, even when her family tells her that it would damage their family name. There are many citizens of South Africa who display virtuous and courageous qualities, each hoping that things will get better as we find our way back to *ubuntu*.

But there is another side to this country which is not to be celebrated.

How is it possible that a country so splendid, with so much potential can also be known as the "rape capital" of the world. A quarter of the men interviewed in a survey admitted to have raped. Fifty people are murdered each day. South Africa has the highest crime rate in the continent, and ranks third in the world with incidents of violent crime. It is the most unequal society in the world, and significantly more unequal than it was when we became a democracy. The wealthy get wealthier and the poor get poorer.

I don't like to read these statistics and I don't like to see the media coverage of rape, violent crimes, poverty and police brutality because it tarnishes the image that I desperately want my country to have. I so much want it to reflect the status we have in cricket and in rugby and in the Oscar wins of Theron and Hood. I want to imagine that it can be the number one country when it comes to safety and security of ordinary citizens, as well as equality among its citizens. But what is reported in the media, and what is reflected in surveys and statistics on violent crime in this country are not disproportionate to what people every day, from all walks of life experience. As South Africans we go through everyday life, celebrating the feats of this country and its citizens, especially in sports, because it has the ability to unify a diverse set of people with a nasty, horrific and violent past.

But we also celebrate the heroics of our sportsmen and women because somehow they make us feel that we can break through the barriers of impossibilities and achieve greatness. They give us hope that we can overcome despite the horrid past and its impact on our individual and national psyche, and the unease of our spirits. That we can transcend the reality of living in one of the most unequal countries in the world, and that things can get better for us as individuals and for the country as a whole. So we live in hope. Hope for a better future is what has brought us so far. Hope is important in moving forward, but hope alone is not enough.

This story is about the life of ordinary people in South Africa. There is nothing that makes the international headlines about rape, molestation, sexual abuse, inequality, femicide, police brutality, dehumanising acts and murder that ordinary citizens do not experience in their everyday lives, and have not been experiencing for a very long time. This book shows what it meant to be a citizen in South Africa in the past and the distant past and what it means today. There is a collective experience of which we are all products, but also a collective hope that we can transcend.

But what is clear is that all South Africans from all walks of life, creeds and races are products of a system existing over an extended time, whose impacts and effects are reflected in the statistics and the media reports. Perhaps all South Africans need to embrace the mirror of yesteryear, and fear it not, for it holds the answers to the questions that we seek today. Questions that, if left unanswered, will still be asked by generations yet to come.

There is a duality to South Africa, as in all of life itself, that is evident, and as stark as the inequality among its citizens. It gives birth to an inspirational sports talent who can also kill his girlfriend; to a naturally gifted leader who can also cheat and fix cricket games; to a brilliant and entrepreneurial businessman who can also beat his wife and children;

to a good educator who abuses and tortures children; to a loving uncle who also touches his nieces inappropriately; to loyal friends of the family that also sodomise the children of their friends; to a colleague whose intellect is so sharp who can also sexually abuse his colleague's daughter; to young talented musicians who gang rape a teenage girl; to children talented beyond measure who choose to keep quiet about what is happening to them in their bedrooms, bathrooms, homes, schools and on the playground, because it all seems normal in this country I call home.

Contents

The birth of sabi

Cultural Legacies are Powerful forces. They have Deep Roots and Long Lives. They persist generation after generation, virtually intact, even as the economic and social and demographic conditions that spawned them have vanished and they play such a role in directing attitudes and behaviour that we cannot make sense of our world without them.

Malcolm Gladwell, *Outliers*

My mother married at a tender age and by the time the middle 1960s came along, she was entering her twenty fourth year of life. The new year was in full swing and she prepared to birth her fourth child. She had previously given birth to two boys and a girl. Her eldest child was a boy who was named after his paternal grandfather.

My paternal grandfather was a proud man who pioneered great things and created wealth without the luxury and backing of ancestral fortunes. He was a visionary and leader with an astute business acumen. My grandfather had an expansive mind and had great command of the material world. He was a polygamist, and had three wives. His first wife, Sarah, was the daughter of an Englishman and an African woman. His second wife, my grandmother, was Sarah's step sister. They shared a mother, but her father was a Chopi, a tribe from Mozambique. His third wife was from an area nearby. He also had children from other women that he did not marry.

My grandfather was born in the Transvaal province, one of the main sites for the protracted and tragic war between the British Empire and the Boers, primarily of Dutch, French and German descent, for control over South Africa, its people and its resources. The war eventually ended with a British victory, but not before they had suffered a number of humiliating defeats by the Boers, whom they outnumbered significantly. For Britain this war was the longest, the most expensive and the bloodiest conflict that they had ever engaged in. It was also at the time the largest number of troops that they had sent overseas, as they had continued to suffer humiliating defeats by the Boers.

It was a horrendous and tragic war where the British in the final analysis employed half a million troops against some sixty thousand Boer troops; they employed the scorched earth military tactics, blockaded food supplies, which led to massive starvation for Africans and for Boers, imprisoned Boer women and children in concentration camps, which resulted in the death of over twenty five thousand of these from starvation, malnutrition and disease. Half of those who died in concentration camps were children.

Large numbers of British troops also died, some seven thousand in battle and at least thirteen thousand from disease. The Boers lost over six thousand troops in battle. At least twenty six thousand Prisoners of War were sent overseas to countries such as Saint Helena, Bermuda and Ceylon.

In separate concentration camps over one hundred thousand Africans were interned. African women were raped by the troops. The death toll for Africans from starvation, malnutrition and disease in concentration camps is not really known, because little attempt was made to keep records of the African population. Both warring factions did not want to arm Africans in the war as they feared for how they would control the native population after the war. But many Africans were inevitably or by default drawn into that war. Some were enlisted, and some, like the Swazi, fought beside the British to try to get their land back from the Boers, and many died. The number of those Africans who died in battle is also not known. Not only were records not kept, but the dead were dumped in mass and unmarked graves.

A total of seventy eight Victoria Crosses were awarded to members of the armed forces. The Victoria Cross is a military decoration, the highest and most prestigious award in the British armed forces for bravery and valour in the face of the enemy, and takes precedence over all other orders, decorations and medals.

By the time of my grandfather's birth, there had been two hundred years of violence that characterised the battle for the soul of South Africa and its resources. In this battle for South Africa the Boers fought and subjugated the African people, the British fought and subjugated the African people, and the Boers and the British fought each other and at the time of the birth of my grandfather, the British fought and subjugated the Boers. Women and children were major casualties in this war; some died and some were dehumanised and raped.

My great grandfather came from England to the Transvaal province of the Union of South Africa towards the end of this violent and tragic war. This province was a key economic province of the Union of South Africa because gold had been discovered. The bloody conflicts had meant that commercial activity had come to a halt. But when the war ended there was much need to stimulate economic activity. The Transvaal and Orange River Colony railways were bought by the British-led Union, and they began to accelerate railway and public works developments to boost economic growth. The Transvaal province was about the size of Great Britain and Ireland, and bordered three countries – Portuguese East India, now known as Mozambique; Rhodesia, now known as Zimbabwe; and Swaziland.

He settled in a town which was formed from the discovery of gold in the late eighteen hundreds. This town is positioned in one of the most beautiful areas in South Africa. It is surrounded by a number of fresh waterfalls and the quality of the water is unrivalled. It is green, everywhere you look, and all year round. By the time my great grandfather arrived in this town, forestation of the area had already begun because wood was needed to support the gold mining industry. Acres upon acres of forests dominate the landscape to this day. There are undulating hills and mountains all around it. It belongs in picture post cards and fits the description of Eden. It is heaven on earth.

But his main interest was in the railway developments that were happening at the time. An expansive railway network was being developed, with the aim of linking this province with other provinces, as well as the neighbouring countries.

We do not know much about my great grandfather, except that he was from England, that he fathered my grandfather, had accumulated wealth through the railway construction industry, and that he is buried in the whites-only cemetery in this town.

My grandfather, however, we do know about. Perhaps it was the reality of growing up without his father, who lived in the same area as he did. He fully embraced the customs, beliefs and traditions of his African mother, whom he grew up with; and he wanted family, a big family. He had three wives and many children. He built an expansive homestead that had three homes to accommodate his wives and their children. His first wife, Sarah, bore him six children, and his second wife, her step sister, bore him seven children, of which my father is the eldest, and his third wife had four children. He believed in big things and plenty.

This philosophy was not wasted on my father, he embraced it fully and set out to create a name for himself and wealth reflected in his possessions and the number of his children. But he was not a polygamist, perhaps because he had experienced first-hand the difficulties of having many wives, had seen the sadness in the eyes of his mother, whom he adored, and witnessed the competition for inheritance when there are so many sons and eldest sons from the different wives. But he did inherit the desire for many children, and would proudly tell of his plan to have fifteen. Perhaps this explains his marriage to a seventeen year old girl, whose hips were reportedly designed for childbearing. Her age would ensure sufficient childbearing years to achieve the requisite number of children without having to marry more than one woman.

My father was born in the mid 1930s and at this time the Union of South Africa had allied with Great Britain against Germany and many South Africans fought in those wars. They also helped to fight and defeat Mussolini in Abyssinia and contributed troops to various allied forces. In the Union itself, the government became preoccupied with categorising and segregating races. Although there was a tension and unease between the British and the Boers in the Union, they were in agreement that the African population should be the source of cheap manual labour. The impact of which is still felt today.

By the 1930s the Boers' National Party was growing in momentum and setting the agenda of the country.

Hertzog, the Prime Minister, put in place laws to entrench segregation, ensuring that Africans and Asians do not take up skilled trades, and limiting access to some areas. But Boers, now known as Afrikaners, were increasingly unhappy that they were fighting with the British in World War II against Germany, whose policies and beliefs mirrored their own vision for South Africa. Many were also not happy that Hertzog had made no real distinction between white people and mixed races. This would usher the formation, in the year of my father's birth, by Daniel Malan of a Purified National Party, which was to take a more hard line approach to segregation, and the real genesis of what was to be known as apartheid was birthed.

My father grew up in this town and when he reached twelve years of age, the year when the National Party established apartheid as a formal policy of the government, he was to move to the Eastern Cape to boarding school.

My eldest brother was born in 1960, followed by my sister in 1962 and the third child arrived in December 1964. Every second year my mother was giving birth. My mother's birth control mechanism was breast feeding; as a result my siblings are more or less two years apart. So when 1966 came along it was two years since my brother before me was born. It was time for my birth into this growing family. The 1960s were a decade of change and rapid growth in my family. My mother was in full swing in birthing children but there were greater changes taking place around the world in this decade.

At the beginning of the 1960s John F Kennedy was participating in presidential debates, winning the presidential race in 1961, pushing for civil right reforms and vowing to land a man on the moon in that decade. It was also the time of the Vietnam war and its accompanying counter culture, anti-war movements, the sexual revolution of the West and the rise of the feminist movement in America. In Europe a rise of more leftist governments in countries like Italy, France and Britain was prominent at the time.

The iconic "I have a dream" speech of the pacifist leader Martin Luther King, which resonates with most people of African descent to this day, also belongs in this period of great change. The assassination of both this great leader and John F Kennedy are key moments of the decade into which I was born. It was a period of rise and fall of great leaders and heroes at the time of my birth and I would witness the same phenomenon in my lifetime.

In the Middle East the "Six Day War" halfway through this decade between Israel and Egypt, Syria and Jordan saw the Israelis gain control of the Gaza Strip, the West Bank, East Jerusalem and the Golan Heights. The shortest war did not result in a peace and fifty years later Israel is effectively still in a state of war. The Middle East did indeed experience great change and by the end of the decade a revolutionary and radical government headed by Col. Muammar al-Qadaffi took power in Libya. The impacts of these changes in the decade of my birth were to find me years later in my early twenties and mid thirties, and in my mid forties I would witness the Arab spring and the fall of Muammar al-Qadaffi.

The winds of change were blowing over Africa too and over a period of eight years between 1960 and 1968, thirty two countries gained independence from their European colonisers.

But in Africa some colonisers did not give up their colonies and stayed for the fight. The wars between the

Portuguese military and emerging nationalist and revolutionary movements in the colonies escalated in this period. It also saw the rise in communist support for armed independence movements in neighbouring countries such as Angola and Mozambique. These wars were to have a direct impact on our lives, as I grew up, especially the Mozambique war.

But those winds of change blowing for freedom and independence did not reach the most southern part of the continent. In fact life took on a very different form in this part of the world. It turned for the worse. Life for black people and anyone supporting liberation ideals and movements became intolerable. The beginning of the decade into which I was born saw the banning of The African National Congress and the Pan Africanist Congress. Perhaps the most brutal act of this decade was the Sharpeville massacre, where the apartheid police killed over sixty people who were demonstrating against pass laws that required all black citizens to carry a passbook to enable them to travel in their own land. My paternal grandmother was to be directly affected by this law.

In March of that year our great leader Robert Mangaliso Sobukwe, leader of the Pan Africanist Congress who led the Sharpeville demonstration, was arrested, and Albert Luthuli, leader of the African National Congress, and later Nobel Peace Prize winner, was arrested with others for openly burning their pass books and inciting riot activity. By the end of March 1960, the apartheid government had declared a state of emergency.

Banned from operating legally in their country of origin, these banned organisations formed militant wings *Poqo* and *Umkhonto we Sizwe* to overthrow the apartheid government. But just three years after their formation, they were dealt a near fatal and crushing defeat when the kingpins like Walter Sisulu and Nelson Mandela were arrested, tried for treason and sentenced to life in prison. It would only be in the birth year of my daughter that Nelson Mandela would be released.

Some leaders did, however, escape, went into exile to other African countries, and began to rebuild. Oliver Reginald Tambo, after whom the current Johannesburg international airport is named, became the president of the African National Congress in exile. Our home was to be a stopover point for some of these freedom fighters in exile.

The master minds behind this offensive that successfully crushed resistance and forced remaining leaders into exile were a certain John Vorster, then Minister of Justice, and General HJ van den Berg, both groomed for pro-Nazi activities in World War II years. In 1966 John Vorster would become the Prime Minister of South Africa.

It is in this year, 1966, that I enter the world, when the Vietnam war is in full swing, Bobby Seale and Huey P Newtown establish the Black Panther Party, the Northern Ireland conflicts begin, and Mao Zedong completes development of China's first atomic bomb. It is also the year, in fact on my date of birth, that Indira Gandhi, a woman, is elected Prime Minister of India. The world's population at this time is about 3.3 billion.

It is a busy decade and a very busy year.

It is now over one hundred years ago that slavery was abolished in the United States of America. Martin Luther King still talks of "A dream" and Mississippi is burning! And in this year of my birth Kwame Ture would make his Black Power speech, which would in my later life resonate deep in my soul.

"This is 1966 and it seems to me that it's 'time out' for nice words...We have to say things nobody else in this

country is willing to say and find the strength internally and from each other to say the things that need to be said."

By all accounts my birth was not a special event. I guess that happens when three others have come before you. My mother recalls that I was born in the early hours of the morning. What I never forget is being told that my father needed confirmation from the nurse that I was actually his, I suppose because I came out looking very different from the daughter that was born before me. To this day I never know if this comment made by my father was a joke. What I do know is, that comment intensified my *sabi*.

By the time of my birth, my father had left his home town more than ten years previously. He had left with the "jacket on his back" from a big family with an ultimate patriarch heading his numerous wives, his many children, workers and his empire. An empire in which my father, although the eldest son of the second wife, would have no say and no benefit.

Large families with many sons competing for favour, status and inheritance rights is a sure recipe for egregiousness. My father's escape from that cess pit allowed him to create his own empire elsewhere, where he would set the rules as patriarch. His journey to this self found wealth would be treacherous and riddled with obstacles and the emotional scars from the need to leave his home would persist with him until his death, and affect his own family in significant ways.

My father was a handsome man. He was tall, dark, brave and had the most charming smile. My mother often spoke of how that smile attracted many women to him during their brief courtship and early wedded time.

He had the gift of speech and could speak many languages. He was a captivating story teller and used parables of ordinary things around him to bring stories and life lessons to life. He was a social being, gregarious and liked having people around him and his home. My father also was an incredible dancer and could sing like Louis Armstrong. He was finely packaged and was respected and feared by many. My father, his home and his business were a magnet for many different people, from varying walks of life and from many countries around the world.

At the time of my arrival into this world that he was creating, my father had bought a house on the outskirts of a medium sized town. He was working as a mechanic for a wealthy man. He used that time to look for opportunities to start a line of work in which he would be boss. My father was not built to work for other people, unless it was a step towards his greater vision. He was born to lead and give instruction and not to take any. At the time of my birth, although living in this town, he had made friends with some fairly wealthy people, and with his typical Libran charm and astute business sense had negotiated a deal in which he would take over an existing business in another town and pay the owner for these rights over a period of time. I was probably around two years old when he moved his family to this place that would define not only the place, but his family and his own life.

I was not born into a poor home. I have no recollection of lack and of not having sufficient resources to do what was necessary to live. My parents did not have it easy when they first met, and had to endure many struggles, but by the time of my birth they were doing all right. In fact what I remember clearly is extended family members, friends or acquaintances of my father coming to him for help. He had an open hand

– a very generous man who helped many people start their own businesses, build their homes and send their children to school. We wanted for nothing material that was necessary to live. My father loved the finer things in life, however. He loved good cars, good furniture and indulged himself and my mother in good watches. He was a stylish man who loved good quality clothes and shoes too.

But those indulgences were not meant for his children. Although we all benefitted from driving in "first in the country" panel vans or luxury cars, my father did not believe in spoiling his children. Everything we needed we had, but he had little regard for indulging children in luxuries. He believed that his children should work for what they had. And work we did. My brothers worked in his businesses from early on in their lives and from the age of ten I was able to drive, worked in his businesses and, because I was an avid reader from a very young age, I was also tasked with the reading kind of work in his businesses. I learnt accounting through my father's Bahia accountant before I did accounting at school. I learnt about negotiating deals during excursions with my father to sales and auctions and I learnt about getting what you want even though the situation seems impossible. My father rarely left an auction or a visit to discuss a business deal empty handed. He was born to do business, to negotiate and to get deals. It is this way that my father built his empire. He believed that you could make money from very simple things in life. Even when we went on holiday, he would always be remarking on a need that was unmet which could result in a business opportunity. I remember one year when I was in university, my father came to Johannesburg with a van filled with cashew nuts that he had got a good price on from one of his many connections in

Mozambique. By the following day, my father had returned back home with much cash in his pocket and an empty van. This was his nature.

We rarely understand how the intricacies of the way we grow up and what we are exposed to define whom we become, no matter what path we eventually take. I thought of this one day when I was interviewed for a director-level position in a national government department. As part of the process candidates were required to take aptitude tests and the test moderators usually gave respondents feedback on the outcome of the tests. I was not surprised by the strategic leadership inclinations he spoke of but what did surprise me was "you should be leading, negotiating and selling". He stated that I had a way-above-average score for selling in particular. That really surprised me because I have always had a particular distaste for selling and stayed away from jobs that required sales. He explained that the national department was offering me a position that required liaising and negotiating with municipalities, various state departments, private sector formations, financiers and community organisations. My particular job would involve selling ideas and pulling the different entities into a singular vision for local economic and social development.

I remember vividly sitting in my car after that test and beginning to understand on a new level how things are connected and tied in some way that most of us do not understand. I had opted for a very different career path from my family but in the final analysis I would be using the same set of skills and aptitudes that I had either learnt or inherited from my father, albeit on a different scale and platform. Over the years I have appreciated more acutely how we are products of our life experiences, but more so, products of where we come from.

Perhaps embracing this point is the first step towards personal freedom. And on reflection as I write, beginning with the man that my father was, highlighting his incredible generosity, talents and achievements demonstrates a step towards the personal freedom I seek. If you had to stop reading this book here you would imagine that my father was so busy being brilliant that he was the ultimate husband and father. That he taught me and my siblings things that would differentiate us from others who perhaps grew up differently and that we all grew up feeling cared for, happy and settled. Stand out we do, but not as you would expect. The reality is quite different, and reality sometimes has a way of spoiling a real good story.

But as I have grown I have come to realise that there are contradictions, dualities and surprises in us all. That each of us always and already has the ability to be both demon and angel, that we can have incredible strengths and display weaknesses in the most bizarre forms, that we can be dull and boring but also creative and intriguing. Mostly I have become aware that all or any of these abilities can be revealed at any time. It is like we are ticking time bombs waiting for life to present us with situations that allow each of these to be manifested.

I have also learnt that you do not know who you are and what you are capable of until the situation arrives when you discover what has been hidden from you, inside of you. Sometimes it takes the unexpected death of a loved one, a moment when watching a riveting movie, an almost irresistible offer to take the easy way out or just a smile from a stranger…but whatever it takes, it is only in those moments that you truly begin to know who you are…for that time, in that situation. In a different time, with a similar situation you might not be what you were in the previous instance.

My father was a hard man. He was particularly hard on his wife and children, and hardest on me. I have scars on my body to attest to the beatings I received as a child. I was beaten so often and so hard that when I was in my early teens I had to be taken to the nearby hospital for treatment and stitches, after the whip he had used had cut too deep into the skin on my thighs. These cuts were so deep that self treatment, at least this time, was not an option. My father took me to the hospital himself and told the doctor I had fallen and that the fence of the vineyard had ripped my skin open. I am sure that the doctor did not believe the story, but this was not the time of children's rights. This was a very different time. Beatings were the order of the day. It was normal that parents beat their children. That was the way to raise kids, no discussion.

I was born into a violent world. I grew up in violence. I live in a violent world. I experienced and witnessed violence in my home, in my school, on the playgrounds, in the streets, among siblings, in relationships, on the television, among parents and everywhere else. In South Africa violence is pandemic, and it is as common a phenomenon and part of our culture and psyche as boerewors, biltong and sunny skies.

But life does offer some respite and happy moments in periods of discomfort and sadness. I was to develop very rewarding friendships with some of the children who lived near my parents' home. The first friend I had was through a chance encounter when I was about three of four years old. I remember that day vividly. I was sitting behind our house alone, crying after a beating from my father, when I heard some rustling in the long grasses and on closer inspection I noticed a girl sitting there. I looked around to see if anyone was looking and hurried to satisfy my curiosity. When I reached her she asked me why I was crying. "Who are you?" I asked. "I am Evy," she said, "And you, what is your name?" I told her my name, but not the reason I was crying. She seemed older than I was, although she told me later that she was the same age. I liked her right away and was drawn to her. I do not know how long I stayed there playing in the tall grasses with her that day, but I enjoyed being with her. We played a game with stones, and every time I managed to catch the right number of stones, she would laugh and reach over to give me a big hug, and say that I was really good with that game. Evy became a friend to me from that day and whenever I could, I would go to play with her, but I made sure that no one ever knew.

Sometimes when I went to meet her, she would come with her cousin and we would all play together. Her cousin Vena was very funny, he always made funny faces and made me laugh. Sometimes when he came along and found me crying he would say, "Do you think your tears can be enough to make a river like that one? What if the crocodiles think your tears are the river and then they come and swim in them?" Then he would lie on the grass and mimic the actions of a crocodile. I always stopped crying when he made these funny movements, because I could imagine the scenes in my mind and they would always make me laugh.

I was very careful that no one saw me go past those trees because my father did not allow us to play near the river, and he would have been angry that I was playing with a boy. This was my secret and I made sure that no one found out.

One day, though, my secret was almost uncovered. Vena made me laugh so much that day that I did not hear my brother calling me. Evy said she heard him calling me and that I should go before I got into trouble, but Vena kept making funny sounds with his mouth so I stayed longer and was rolling around the grass laughing with him. Almost too late I heard footsteps and saw a shadow. "Where are you?" he said. Evy and Vena quickly got away, but I was still laughing. "What are you doing here and what are you laughing at?" my brother said. I tried to stop laughing but I could not, and then he said, "Dad has been calling you for so long, you better stop laughing!" Later my brother told my mother that he thought I was going mad because I was laughing to myself. But I never told them why I was laughing that day.

Outside of my friendship with Evy and her cousin, the world around me was violent. Police were violent to black men, women and children alike with no consequence to them. Men were violent to women with no consequence. Teachers were violent to pupils with no consequence and parents were violent to their children with no consequence. In fact it was common practice that you would bring the branch from the tree or the belt or the whip that would be used to beat you up. This was not the time of the Human Rights bodies. It was a free for all.

Is it possible that "no consequence" can become a culture or an acquired trait of a people down the line? Are we perhaps reaping the consequence of "no consequence"?

My mother suspects that my youngest brother is the one who got rid of that gun that stayed in a drawer next to my father's side of the bed. I hated that gun so much. I could always see when that thing in my father that caused him to want to lash out at someone was building inside of him. It was as if he had something in him that he needed to get out of himself and the only way he could quieten it was to hit someone. And sometimes when that thing inside of him was so desperate to come out, he would take the gun and walk around the house threatening to do unthinkable things. He held the gun against my mother's forehead many times. But one day when he held it against her head, I noticed that my mother seemed to have no fear, it was as if she was resigned to death, and perhaps she longed for it. My father was raging all sorts of accusations at her for something that I cannot even remember and she just sat there with peace all over her countenance. I am glad someone got rid of that gun, because one day he would not have managed to satisfy the thing in him that needed to come out without pulling that trigger. Maybe that thing inside becomes greedier and greedier and needs so much more to satisfy it.

There are often reports in our media of a man who kills his wife and children and then turns the gun on himself. Each time I see these reports I get a shiver down my spine because I know how close our family came to being just one of the many families who have found this fate.

I noticed too that my father was quite unsure of my mother. It did not seem to matter that she had defied her own family's preferences to be with him, or that she stayed through very difficult times, or that he had a way to get her to laugh or that he could arouse her interest in some topic or story he told specifically for her ear. He always thought that she would rather be with somebody else. He accused her of having an interest in other men, often. When I first watched the *Othello* production that stars Kenneth Branagh and Lawrence Fishburne, I felt that I was watching a scene from my home.

Maybe he did not believe he deserved her. Maybe he had tried so hard to achieve and to be somebody, despite his colour and the currency it represents, and after he had the power, the prestige and the wealth he still could not believe that he had done enough, or was enough, to keep her. Maybe that thing inside of him,

28

that restless thing, just could not give him the peace to just be.

There is no race or class in South Africa that is immune to this dis-ease. It is handed down from generation to generation; the way my great grandfather handed it down to my grandfather and my grandfather to my father, and my father in turn to his children. This dis-ease is not reserved for a specific class or race.

Sometimes I look at the societies of both the United States of America and South Africa and I see glaring similarities. High violence rates and high prison populations. These countries have both had a prolonged and protracted system of institutionalised dehumanisation, discrimination and violence. I wonder if just maybe this can explain the source of this violence. Do these societies have an internal anger and rage that finds expression in the horrific acts of madness that "shock" us when done on a mass scale and make international headlines in the media and when either the victim or the perpetrator is a famous person?

I received many beatings in my home, mostly from my father, twice from my mother. My mother was not the hitting type, I guess that was my father's job. She had a particular style for her beatings, though. One of my father's businesses involved selling motor spare parts; my mother managed that store and to this day I do not know anyone who knows car and truck spare parts better than she does. She would give us the keys to open the shop and tell us specifically which fan belt to fetch. "Just bring me a fan belt. A Datsun 1400 fan belt. Yes, let me show you what I can do with it." I can't remember if the second beating was justified, but at that time I certainly thought that this one was. I have always been inquisitive and curious about various things and fire was the topical curiosity for me at the time. I was playing with matches and successfully managed to burn much of my parents' and brother's clothes as well as fine furniture pieces. I knew I was in trouble and I remember while my mother was beating me I was asking myself, "Why are you so naughty?" The truth is, that was one beating that I not only felt I deserved, but I didn't really feel much pain, even though the marks on my body later would attest to a different reality.

Perhaps the most humiliating beating came from a stranger. I had just finished university and I was driving my first car in a business and college district in Johannesburg. I mistakenly drove into a turning lane, but proceeded driving straight, rather than turning left. When I stopped my car at the next traffic lights I noticed a huge Afrikaner man get out of his car and before I knew what was going on he was beating me through the car window. For a long time after that I would not dare drive with my window open.

The strangest thing about that incident is the reaction of people at the scene. Nobody made a sound and nobody came to my rescue. This is what happens when violence is so ingrained in a people's psyche. Here was a grown big man beating a twenty year old woman and nothing happened. No consequence. I do remember him saying in Afrikaans, "You kaffir, can't you f...g drive properly!" He said many other things that I didn't comprehend at the time he was abusing me or any other time after that. But that was a very humiliating experience for me. You get beaten for making a mistake in a turning lane? You are beaten for just being black? Reducing mistakes on the road is something I can do something about. But I couldn't do anything about being black. All I had to do was get up in the morning and I was guilty.

The word "kaffir" is a derogatory term used by some white people and some fair skinned people to refer to Africans and dark skinned people in South Africa. It is the equivalent to the word "nigger" that is used to describe Africans that were taken from the continent, especially in the Unites States of America. That word brings up extreme feelings in people in this country because it summarises in a word the dehumanisation that Africans have been subjected to for hundreds of years, the consequences of which we live every day. We heard our parents being called by that name when they were pushed around, beaten and disrespected. We experienced the use of that word directed at us when we were beaten, and today we live the consequences of hundreds of years of what that word means.

I feel sad that our brothers and sisters across the oceans choose to use the n-word when referring to each other. Perhaps it is the disconnection from the motherland, its people and its traditions and cultures and perhaps even the feeling of being a foreigner in the country of your birth. I don't know. But when Idris Elba said "I don't use the n-word, I am an African", what he did was remind us that we are Africans, and that we do not have to adopt the derogatory labels that our oppressors have used to refer to us. Perhaps we should proudly call ourselves Africans and begin to show the world how they need to refer to us, with respect for who we are. By using that word Elba honours the memory of those who sacrificed so much so he can have the opportunities that he has today to shine on the big screen. He makes a choice in that statement, to affirm the dignity of Africans. But mostly he honours himself.

If you have been assaulted and dehumanised and that word, or in our case, "kaffir", is used to show you why you are being dehumanised, it is perhaps inane to say "it is just a word", because it is not just a word. It carries the bloodstains of generations who have come before us.

I pray I never hear my children use those words when they refer to each other, or anyone else who is black and/or African. I hope like Idris Elba they would proudly say, "I am an African." It would be disrespectful to themselves as Africans, and to those who were beaten, tortured, deprived of sleep and water, lynched and killed so that they may be free. The ultimate question for me is, when you have the power to influence and change mindsets that have been formed over hundreds of years, how do you choose to use that power?

I don't deal well with powerlessness. I don't know if anyone else can say it is something that they deal well with. But I have always felt that I have a particular intolerance and abhorrence for powerlessness and lack of options. Perhaps it is my innate character trait or one that was formed in growing up with a father like mine. He always felt that there was something you could do about anything. The truth is, I witnessed him for most of his life doing something about something or anything or everything. That philosophy permeates who I became and who I still am in most circumstances. There are only a very few instances where this philosophy abandons me.

If there is a problem, you do what is necessary to fix it. If your sister needs help, you find a way to help her. If there is a difficult supplier, you go and negotiate and if that doesn't succeed, you find another. If there is a pain in your hand you take medication to take the pain away. If there is a lack, you work harder till you can take care of the lack. If you have a problem with someone, you approach them and talk about it. The key here is that you have the power to do something about something. But when the problem is your skin colour, there is nothing you can do about it. Nothing! You are powerless and subject to the violence of a stranger because you woke up in the morning.

I witnessed my father, a strong and proud man, being insulted, threatened and pushed around by a very young white policeman when I was younger. One day my father was driving to Johannesburg when the car was pulled over and searched. I could see that every inch of my father's body and mind wanted to retaliate but he felt powerless in that moment. At one point he instinctively moved his arm to defend himself, and the policeman showed "the kaffir" who was in charge. Violence impacts both the victim and the perpetrator, and perhaps it is not surprising that violence is found in the homes of the white man as well as the black man in this country. They learnt to respond to fear and the unknown with violence and they learnt to express their anger through violence.

In this country, even dogs were trained to bark at and attack black people. Black South Africans know exactly what it feels like to be walking down a street in a white suburb. My aunt once responded to an advertisement in the classifieds to buy a dog, and because she sounds Caucasian on the phone, the seller told her she would be very happy with the dog because it can "deal" with black people and told her that it was trained specifically for this purpose. They never realised that the enemy was never black people, but rather a system that we are all products of.

Perhaps the distaste I have had for powerlessness formed early on in my life. The *sabi* that there is something wrong with you, you don't really understand why, but you are sure that you can't do anything to fix it. I have an obsession for options and on reflection I guess this has its roots in the fear of powerlessness. If you have options, you minimise powerlessness. Study hard, get educated, earn good money so that you don't have to be subjected to other people's fancies and asinine prejudices. My conscious mind cannot explain when these philosophies developed, but looking back I find evidence from a young age of my attempting to build options.

One memory makes me laugh today, but you can be sure I was not laughing much back then. My mother's family are very fair skinned. My maternal grandmother was an Irish/English woman, complete with long black and grey hair with a big mole to boot on her cheek, and my maternal grandfather, who died the year I was born, was also fair skinned. I am told that my maternal grandfather has some black blood in him, but he looked white. So together these fair skinned people made some very fair skinned children. Some of my mother's siblings married white people, but my mother was taken by the pursuits of this handsome, charming, charismatic, well dressed, strong and formidable black man who was my father. There was also probably an invisible sign on his forehead, that said "I have a plan, I will take care of you and our children". My father was quite the catch.

My eldest sister was not only fair skinned, she had Caucasian hair and green eyes to complete the look. And many of my maternal cousins looked that way. I was different, black with African hair. In that time black and African hair equalled ugly. Actually, it probably still does, if you consider the number of weaves which are sold even when the economy is in dire straits. It didn't matter that I had my father's smile, or the defined jaw and the slanted eye from my mother. What always first defined you was the colour of your skin. It didn't matter that I loved to sing, had a good knack for languages, had an incredible memory for things I deemed important or that I loved being alone. All other characteristics both internal and external were secondary or, more precisely, invisible, always subject to what colour you are. By the same token no one noticed the distinctly African nose that some of my whiter family had, even though that kind of nose, like mine, was the butt of jokes many people make about black people. This powerlessness against skin colour made me very resourceful at alternatives and options. I often retreated into my own world, which had its own rules and currencies and revenges. In this world, which I began to create very early on, the currency was intelligence.

One Sunday afternoon we went to visit one of my maternal aunts. Her children looked like my sister. As is tradition in our family, when you visit family you greet them with a kiss to the lips and/or a hug. When we visited my father's siblings, this cultural act was done without incident, because they all looked like my father. But when we visited my mother's side, it was always humiliating for me. Some of my cousins wouldn't kiss me until an adult would point out to them not to be rude. And when they were compelled to greet me properly and in family custom style they would immediately wipe their mouths in my presence. As if my blackness would rub off on them.

At first this made me feel very sad, but after a while it did not bother me so much. When I would play with Evy and Vena, we would act out elaborate and funny scenes and make fun of them. Vena would tell me to

35

kiss his hand, and when I did he would mimic wailing sounds and say, "Look, I am turning black...blacker!" Or he would make jokes about my having special powers to make people turn into different colours, and say "please touch me and make me turn green like the leaves on the papaya tree". Vena liked acting and making funny faces that made me laugh. I appreciated the time I spent with my friends, because I always felt better. I thought about my "powers" and often wondered what would happen if I used my magic powers to turn my cousins black. When I was with my friends I really did believe that it was the world that was crazy and not me.

When my father met my mother he was not wealthy, and his wealth, like that of most men I know who are wealthy or successful, only came when he was settled, married and the children were on their way. Women really do have a way of separating the boys from the men, no matter what their age or economic standing is at the time. And sometimes when women are irresistibly drawn to men whom they know are really "boys", it is then that "Project Fix Them and Mould Them" begins. However, if it is the real deal, women know that their only role is to provide the environment in which that man can manifest in the physical world all that he already is inside, and when that happens she and her children will be taken care of. But I guess it is also those men, who know who to choose, themselves choose the real deal. My father would not have achieved what he did without my mother, this I *sabi*, without a doubt. As Thomas Sankara would say, "Women hold up the other half of the sky."

My father often told us that a man's greatest quest in life is first to find a purpose which when he wakes up every day he wants to do. It is from this purpose that his footprint is to be made. And secondly, to find the right woman to partner him, and it is from this union where his footprint on the world and wealth is sustained. He would tell us elaborate stories about formidable men he knew who got the first thing right but failed at the second, resulting in a failure or loss of the first. I was never sure if my father was making up these stories or if he was trying to instil these ideas into my brothers' psyches, but sometimes we would be driving through the main city and he would see someone and say "You see there is another one...The man was great, but look at him now walking like a lost soul...everyone told him to leave that woman alone."

In these moments I wondered whether it was the same for women. If a woman found a purpose for herself and found the right partner, would it produce the same results? I certainly have seen women with indomitable spirits and robust plans for their future get derailed because the men in their lives were not suitable for the trajectories that these women's lives could take. I have seen women enter boardrooms wearing too much make-up in order to hide bruises, or wearing long sleeves to mask the signs of violence in their homes. I have even witnessed women who speak out against women and child abuse in post apartheid South Africa who experience this brutality at home.

But my father was an impactful person with lots of stories, many of them elaborate and colourful. Long after his death, if you met anyone who had known him, they would tell you a story about a story he had told them, and their re-telling of those tales always made them cry and laugh. I figured many cried because they realised what he really was and how rare it is to meet real impactful characters in one's lifetime, and laughed because he had a way of telling stories, that no matter how serious the story, they would always make you laugh. Sometimes he reminded me of Vena.

Many people throughout my life have thought of me as a very serious person. Perhaps that is what I portray. They do not know or see the high degree of jest in the lenses through which I view the world around me. Vena taught me how to do that from a very early age and it has helped me to see the slapstick side of the events and people I have encountered. There is an entire series of comedy shows that Vena and I performed throughout my growing years that perhaps should not be reserved for us alone. But I am also very jealous of my experiences with my friends and have never been comfortable to let anyone else experience them but us.

There are only a handful of people who have referred to me as being "funny". They have perhaps come the closest to knowing this side of who I am, or at least had a really small peek into what may lie inside of me. Most don't come that close or perhaps I don't allow them to. I have always felt invisible in the world around me and misunderstood, and my own character has perhaps developed in response to that.

But many people actually believe they know me, and go to great lengths to convince me and mostly themselves of how well they know me. "I have studied you and I know you" is a very common phrase I have gotten to hear in my life. I have watched some people sloganise or paraphrase my life into words that make sense to them. Some brush aside my entire life with a dismissive and condescending wave of a hand, each vowing that they know what is wrong with me and exactly what I need to be better or to be fixed. In these moments I see the look of a woman I once knew who went to incredible lengths to try to fix me.

I sometimes stand back and look at these people and imagine them spending one week as me. I wonder if they would handle the smugness and "holier than thou" looks that I see reflected in their eyes or in the dismissive quotes when they summarise my entire being into a half thought out sentence. In these cases, when I see that there is no hope, after a few attempts to adjust the lenses through which they see me, I enter my silence and sorely miss my friends Evy and Vena. These are the people who know me well, and actually think I am okay.

Amagugu

I was four years old when I was sent to live with my paternal grandmother and to begin my primary schooling. In South Africa, many children start school at the age of six or seven. But I began school at the tender age of four. This town to which I was sent for schooling was my grandfather's and father's birthplace, and the place my great grandfather had moved to when he arrived from Great Britain. It was also the place from which my father had fled in the early hours of the morning, to start a new life elsewhere. And at that age I was not to learn about how he left, but would certainly be exposed to the reasons for his having fled.

I lived with my grandmother in her house, and all of her own children, like my father, had moved to towns far away from this place. The children of the first wife were, however, living there and they had their own houses where they lived with their spouses and children. My grandmother did not live a very privileged life despite my grandfather's wealth, and she would bake Swazi buns, and *amagwinya*, also known as fat cakes, for us to sell at school. We did, however, get to meet her family and two of her brother's children lived with her at the time.

I enjoyed living with my grandmother. I was named after her and I think she liked me. I would often look at my grandmother and see something familiar in her eyes; I did not know what it was. Sometimes she would catch me staring at her and say, "*Ubonani wena?*" meaning "What is it that you see?" I would normally just start laughing and run outside. I loved my grandmother and I do not have a memory of her trying to fix me.

Her house was divided into three separate stand alone parts. There was a main house that had a lounge, bedrooms and a dining area, a second part which housed the kitchen and a pantry, and the third part housed the bathroom. The door of the kitchen faced the back door of the main house. The kitchen part was quite big and had a stove that used wood and coal, and my grandmother or her helper would prepare meals there. From the kitchen door, when facing the main house, the bathroom area was located on the right side of the kitchen area.

In the early evenings my grandmother insisted that we bath, and one day it was lightning while I was bathing. She had always told me that I was not to touch the taps, as the lightning would strike me and I would surely die. I don't know what came over me, but I kept my hands on the taps and just before one of the strikes lit the bathroom something happened to me but I do not remember much after that. My next memory of this incident is feeling acute pain in my legs. I realised that my Gogo, which is what we called her, was beating me with a wooden plank. I started screaming in protest, when she said *"Yima ntombi wami, ngizokhipa umlilo"*. It was a painful exercise but my Gogo explained that she was removing the lightning from my body. I saw fear in her eyes that day, and she made me promise that I would never touch taps when it was lightning ever again. "Yebo Gogo," I said, still in shock.

I liked living with my Gogo, and she would always smile when she saw my sister and me in our school uniforms. I did not have friends even though there were many children in that area. They were the offspring of my father's half brothers and sisters but I never really felt part of them, and also my grandmother did not encourage me to play with them. My sister schooled with me at the time, but like my father she was gregarious and got along well with the other children there. So when I was not in school I spent most of the time with my grandmother or played alone on the side of the house where the laundry was hung.

But that playing area was soon to become the site of something ugly and I avoided it after the incident. Gogo's helper, Busi, was doing the laundry outside and she started to cough. The cough got louder and louder and it scared me so much that I ran to the kitchen to tell my grandmother. She hurried out with me to see what was happening. When she saw what was happening she told me to go back into the house and not to look. I tried to look, but my grandmother's niece picked me up and took me into the house and remonstrated with me for not listening. I wish I was not there that day, because the stories that I heard after that incident kept me awake at night. I heard my Gogo and her brother talk about Busi's *nyoka,* her internal snake which was trying to come out and was choking her to death. I heard my grand uncle saying that if it came out then she would die because no person can live without their *nyoka.* I heard speculative stories about what she could have done to anger her *nyoka.* I was scared, and all attempts to get my grandmother to explain these things to me were met with cautionary words about "listening to big people's stories". I was afraid to sleep at night because my very over-active imagination would go into overdrive. What if I did something to upset my *nyoka*? Would it choke me? I imagined it must have been very painful to vomit a snake. The imagery was too much for my young brain to deal with, and I was petrified. When I returned home to my parents' home for holidays, I asked my mother about it, and she dismissed it and said that Busi was just ill and that there are no snakes inside people, and warned me not to listen to such stories. I was not satisfied, and I asked Evy whether she had ever heard about this. She assured me that there are no snakes living inside people and that the older people said that to get their children to eat their vegetables. That is all I needed to hear and I dismissed them as old people's stories. Vena also helped me to get over that imagery in my mind by converting it into a funny scene that made me laugh.

I loved my grandmother and she liked to tell stories that would captivate me, but some of them were real life stories. She would often warn me to be careful when she sent me to get something from Aunt Catherine's house, which was visible from the window at the back of the kitchen. She told me that this aunt, who was a step sister to my father, had held her own daughter's hand on a hot stove because she had suspected her of stealing. The fear of being burnt on the hot stove made me very careful when I went to that aunt's house, and I never stayed long there.

My grandmother loved going to church too. She wore the traditional church clothes, a white cap, red jacket and black skirt, every Sunday when she went to church. She never missed going to church and I would go along and mostly watch my Gogo in church as she sang. I was not really aware of God in those times, it was something that I watched people do. I got to learn a song that my grandmother sang a lot walking to and from church, and when I knew the words I would sing along with her. She never looked happy when she sang that song but I sang it with her because she sang it so often.

Amagugu aleliswe
Ayosale matunweni
Ngiyolala ngingetwa
Ethunweni lami
Ngiyolala ngingetwa

Many times she would be sitting alone on her veranda, which was on the front side of the main house, and sing that song with a distant look and sadness in her eyes. As I grew older and understood the lyrics of that song, I realised that my grandmother, like me, had a sadness and I wondered if she *sabi*'d, like I did. Later my father's eldest sister told me that my grandmother became the second wife of my grandfather because her half sister, the first wife, needed someone to help her clean and take care of her children. My grandfather married her to be a maid to his first wife.

I would see my parents and other siblings three or four times a year during school holidays, and that pattern would continue until I graduated from university. During the first part of my schooling, I lived with my grandmother for two years and my father's second sister for another two years in two different towns in the Eastern Transvaal province.

The first time I got to hear the word "rape" spoken was when I lived with my aunt. The houses where people lived in these townships were very small and it was very easy to hear what the adults were talking about. I heard a conversation between her and some neighbours in which my aunt was crying in solidarity with a neighbour who had been raped by a family member. I listened to the conversation intently and could not really make out what it was that the man had done to this woman. But I had a sense from the way she was crying that it was something that made both her and my aunt feel very bad. They spoke of him liking to touch girls inappropriately, and I thought it must be different from the way that some of our uncles would make comments and touch our breasts, and make jokes about how our "guavas" were growing. This they

44

always did in the open, so it must have been a normal thing that uncles do with their nieces, although it never felt right to us.

As I grew up, though, I would realise that rape was a common occurrence all around me. I would learn that the people around me whom I love are capable of such horrendousness and I would learn that this too, can be passed down from generation to generation.

I discovered Pentecostal Churches when I went to live with my father's second sister. She belonged to a church which was in the residential area where she lived and she would go to church a lot. Every Sunday she would take my sister and me along with her. The language medium in this place was Afrikaans, which was different from the SiSwati and English that we grew up with. I had to adjust to learning in a new language at school, and at church we would sing songs in Afrikaans. Two songs from those years that will not leave my memory and that of my sister are *Ek en my huis, ons sal die Here dien*, which translates into "Me and my house, we will serve the Lord". My aunt sang that song a lot in the house. The other song was also sung much in the church that we went to:

Wat sal jy maak, die dag is Jesus kom?
Die deure is gesluit, dan staan julle buite kant.

Meaning, "What will you do, the day when Jesus comes, the doors will be locked, then you will be left outside". This song normally sent shivers down my spine, because I always imagined that if Jesus did not like me the way other people appeared not to like me, then I would be standing outside those doors and would be lost forever. Sometimes I thought that if I sang it a lot, then Jesus would recognise my efforts and not leave me stranded on the other side.

During this time of my father's life he was not very much into church business. He did go to church but it

45

did not play a significant role in our lives; that would come later. My aunt made various attempts to get him and her other siblings to "convert" to Pentecostalism, but my father resisted until much later. So when my sister and I would return home and sing these songs, they were often met with sniggers from my father.

We belonged to the Methodist Church and it was a peaceful and quiet church where people spoke in a steady manner and sang hymns from a hymn book. There was not much ritual in the church and they spoke much about love and helping other people and striving to live life like Jesus did. Our church was also a mix of people from different countries and different races. What I remember most about the visits to the church we went to when we were at home was the peace that surrounded that church. Everyone seemed happy and at peace in that church and even my father's strictness and harshness seemed subdued on the way back from church. Because we lived eighty kilometres away from the Methodist Church, my father would stop in the town and buy ice creams for us to eat on our ride back home, or if we had not finished the cooking before leaving for church he would buy a bucket of Kentucky Fried Chicken for his very large family. It was also customary to buy the Sunday newspapers, and my father would enlist us to read the newspapers for him.

But my aunt's church was located in a township where only people of mixed race lived. Most people spoke Afrikaans there. The church had very passionate and vocal pastors, who were excitable and preached at the top of their lungs about God and about mending your ways before Jesus came. There was a desperation in the voices in the sermons and in the prayers. The singing and band playing was loud and people danced around so much, and some of them appeared to be in a trance-like state. Some people would speak in different languages; this was called "praying in the spirit" or "speaking in tongues". And sometimes another member of the church would come to the front of the church to interpret what the other had said via a prophecy, so that the rest of the church could understand what message God had for them that day. It was different, very different from the church we went to at my parents' home, and very different from my grandmother's church, which was also much quieter, although my grandmother always seemed very sad when she left the church.

Doctor Fixit

I was nine years of age when I left my aunt's place and the sounds of the Pentecostal church and Afrikaans behind. My father sent me to school in Harding, a town in the Natal province, which is in the most eastern part of the country. My elder sister and I would undertake an eight hundred kilometre journey, normally accompanied by my father and mother, and we were left for three or four months at a time, only returning during the school holidays. We lived with a couple who had three children, all attending the school we had been enrolled in. They were also Christian and attended the local Anglican church. This church was different from all the other churches I had encountered before. It was not really a loud church, but it had rituals that involved the priest's burning incense and many of the prayers were read from a book.

This period of my life was a torturous one for me, from beginning to end. No child should be subjected to such intolerable cruelty, ever. But this was not the time of human rights culture or organisations.

Harding was a town close to the Drakensberg mountains, and in winter it was very cold. Snow would often fall on those cold winter days and nights. I had never seen snow before and had no idea how cold snowy conditions could be. There are no memories of that time which are joyous for me, none at all. Not the time that I was in Harding, and especially not the time when I returned home. Each place presented a kind of hell for me.

Her name should have been Cruella de Ville. She was bitter, unhappy and very cruel. During my lifetime I have met women who are very bitter and I have seen the venom inside of them spill from their nostrils and mouths. Some have had very big and many disappointments throughout their lives and perhaps they just have found no place where they can experience happiness or where they feel loved and accepted. But this woman was a teacher, she had a family, three children and a husband and she is to this day the most bitter and cruellest woman I have met in my life. Perhaps something had happened to her that made her see the world as a cruel and sad place.

My sister and I had very clear duties in the house each day. We were the help. We cleaned, scrubbed, cooked every day. We had to awake before the whole family each morning, go outside, clean the dog kennel, cook maize meal porridge, and clean the house. Then we needed to get ready for school. We would walk to the school, which was not too far from the house in which we stayed. After school we would walk back to the house and begin our after school duties. This involved cooking for their dogs, cleaning the parts of the house that were not cleaned in the morning, cleaning the windows and the yard and cooking for the evening meal. We worked every day. In the evening we would do our homework, and then go to sleep until the early hours of the morning, when we awoke to start our day jobs. I was nine years old when we went to live with this woman.

We were not allowed to mess up, and if we did, we got into much trouble. Cruella belonged in Guantanamo Bay as their chief torturer. The American Government would have had a prized possession, as she would have extracted the information they required from their inmates. The torture took various forms and the most malicious, callous and brutal of them were reserved for me. I was her punching bag, the butt of her jokes and the guinea pig of her torture methods. To this day I do not know if my fear of dogs emanated from being ordered to sleep in the dog kennel, outside in freezing cold weather, or whether I naturally fear dogs. I remember the first time it happened, it was one of the days I was deemed to be too lazy, because I was not cleaning to the standards that she required.

I worked every day and very hard, and I got my homework done to a high quality each day, but for some reason Cruella felt I was very lazy. One day she told me that she would be taking me to the doctor to cure this "laziness of yours". When we got to the doctor, Cruella informed him that I was very sluggish, always dragging my feet and very lazy, and that he needed to check what was wrong with me. I never got to find out what was wrong with me, but I received an injection that day, and each week I would go back to that doctor to receive shots to cure my laziness.

Later on I would ponder why people, especially Cruella and my father, thought I was lazy. Perhaps they expected me to be busy, working. Perhaps it was what my colour represented. So even when I had finished my chores and would go into the yard to play, I was probably acting outside of what my role was. Sometimes my father would return from work and find me sitting outside on the veranda reading. Instinctively he would say something like "You just sitting there, did you clean the windows?" and when I told him I had, he would find something else for me to do. Cruella was the same. As a result I would find places in the house where I was not easily spotted, mainly under the ironing deck, and there I would read. Sometimes I would be lost in the world of the story I was reading and not hear anyone enter the room. A few times my mother found me reading under that ironing deck, but she never spoke of it, but when she left the room, she would tell me not to forget to finish the ironing. I suppose she understood that part of me, because she also loved to read.

One day when I was walking to school I saw a girl who looked like Evy entering the school yard. I walked faster to try to catch up with her, but she disappeared in the crowds that were entering their classrooms. I could not concentrate all morning at school, waiting for the bell to ring so I could go and check if my eyes were not deceiving me. When the bell rang I ran out of the classroom and began searching for her. I could not find her and decided to go to the administration block to enquire whether a new girl had started school that day. Just as I started to walk up the stairs of the administration block I heard a very familiar voice behind me. I turned around and saw Evy, Vena and her other cousin, Luthi, standing there, smiling at me. I hurried down the stairs and threw my arms around Evy. I was so happy to see my friend. Vena was laughing as usual, and Luthi wore his normal stern face. But I could see that they were all very happy to see me.

We sat at the pond of the school and I asked them what they were doing here in this very cold place. Evy explained that her mother had got an opening in the school for them and that they were going to be term-boarders with a woman who was living on her own in a big house. I was very pleased that they were there because I missed them those first weeks after moving to this place. But my excitement was to increase when we walked home after school and Evy showed me where they were staying. They were my next door neighbours! This place may not be that bad after all, I thought to myself.

One afternoon my sister and I went to eat lunch together during the school lunch break. We opened our lunch tins to take out our sandwiches and there was a horrible smell coming from it. When we opened the sandwiches we saw that there was some black stuff in between the two slices of bread, we did not know what it was, but it smelled so bad. We did not have lunch that day, but when we were walking back from school with Cruella's daughter we noticed that she had something different on her bread and that there was nothing rotten or smelly in her sandwich. We commented on this and asked her if she knew what the black stuff was in our sandwiches. There are many things that you can remember in the course of your life, but there are those things or moments that you never forget, they are never even filed or shelved in your memory bank, instead they are there as if they happened ten minutes ago. This is one of those memories.

I do not know what came into our very young brains that we asked that question. I do not believe we knew what Cruella was capable of until that day. When we returned to the house, her daughter informed her that we had complained about our lunch. She first did her normal punching bag routine on us, and when she was done she told us to do our chores, and we went to clean. I thought we had received the punishment for that crime. I was mistaken. When we finished cleaning, she called us into her kitchen and I noticed that she had filled the kitchen table with all sorts of food, some cooked and some not, some fresh and some not. Then she told us that we were greedy and today she would teach us a lesson. She told us to start eating all the food on that table, and that we were not to stop until the table was clean. I started crying, saying that we were sorry and that we would not be greedy again, and that we would eat anything that she gave us for lunch. She landed a few punches to my body and told me to "shut up and start eating".

My sister and I began to eat. We ate and ate, until we reached various stages of nausea. When we could eat no more, she'd tell us to drink warm water, to put our fingers in our mouths and we would start to vomit. When the vomiting sessions were over, we had to continue eating. We ate, felt nauseous, drank warm water, put our fingers in our mouths and vomited over and over and over and over and over again until that food, that could feed twenty very hungry grown men, was finished. Of course there was much crying accompanying this torture. I became physically weak from the self induced and forced vomiting spells that had sapped all the energy from me. She hurled a few profanities at me and pushed the broom handle in my throat, without finesse, to initiate the vomiting.

It was painful. I now noticed that there was much blood in the bucket that was the receptacle of all the regurgitated food, tears and blood. The broom handle had really injured my throat. I did not know what to do, but in that moment I felt like dying. My grandmother had just died a few months earlier and I wanted to be with her so badly. I started to think about how to die and that was the last thing I remembered about that incident.

The next time I recall about that time is when myself, Evy and Luthi were sitting near the fence. I could not tell them what had happened but Luthi said he knew and Evy nodded in agreement. She held me in her arms and never spoke a word, she just held me, but I could see what I should have been feeling in her eyes, and by the tension of her grip on me. She cried for me for I could not. I saw the horror, humiliation and feeling of utter worthlessness in her eyes. In Luthi's eyes I saw the rage. The three of us never spoke about that incident. There are some things that you never have to or should ever speak about, for the mouth cannot ever articulate or form the appropriate words to describe what the mind and soul itself cannot comprehend.

A few days after this incident Cruella had a very nasty fall from the chair she was standing on. She was in much pain and I ran over to help her up. It was difficult for her to get up, and she was remonstrating as I tried to help her to her feet. I called for her eldest son, who helped her to her room. For weeks after that she was grimacing and looking very uncomfortable from the pain of that fall. She also struggled to walk properly and limped around for some time.

The meanness was unequalled. One Sunday morning, my sister and I together with her daughter went to their Anglican church. On returning from church, Cruella asked me where my school shoes were. I told her that they were in the room and she requested me to fetch them and show them to her. I searched the room and could not find my school shoes. I searched inside the house and then went to look in the shed outside. I saw Luthi there and told him I was looking for my shoes and could not find them. Luthi said she must have taken them, but I was not sure. I eventually returned to the house and informed her that I did not know what had happened to them, but swore that I had put them in the shoe rack in the bedroom. She hurled her usual insults at me and told me what the punishment for my recklessness would be. I was to walk barefoot to school every day until I found my shoes, so that I could learn what fibbing and carelessness feels like.

The walks to and from school and the six hours of school each day was torture. The town was so cold that each classroom was fitted with a furnace to keep it warm. But even with those furnaces, my feet would be frozen. The walks outside of the classroom and to and from the house where we stayed were pure hell, and my feet developed deep fissures and bled from being exposed to the harsh elements. In the afternoons when I was cleaning the outside yard, Evy would come to the back yard and apply Vaseline to my feet and rub them. Whenever she left to go back to her place, she would hold my face between her hands and look in my eyes and not say a word. I knew what she was saying, there was no need for words.

I spent more than two months without school shoes. One day her son told me where my shoes were. He said he had seen his mother hiding them in her bedroom cupboard when I had gone to church. That presented a quandary for me, what should I do? If I take the shoes and start wearing them, then she would know that I had been "scratching" around in her room. If I told her that her son told me where they were then he would be in trouble. I thought for days how to deal with this *impasse*. One day, when she was out of the house I went to fetch the shoes from her cupboard, and hid them in the outside shed where our empty suitcases and the garden tools were kept. The shoes stayed there for weeks while I continued to walk barefoot in the icy conditions. I would contemplate the next move, but each time thought it best to keep them hidden there, mainly because I did not want to be beaten up by my father for losing my shoes. I figured the best plan was to take them with me when my father fetched us for the school holidays, and return with them as new shoes my father had bought, to replace the ones that I had "lost". I would just suffer the rest of the school term barefoot. Luthi disagreed with me on this course of action; he felt I should just take the shoes and start wearing them. He constantly urged me to wear them, but I could not. That was my plan, but as fate would have it, my plans were disrupted.

It was on a Saturday morning while I was hanging the laundry in the back yard that she called out for me. She asked me if I had been scratching around in her room. I said, "No, I have not been scratching in your room." She said, "Don't you lie to me! I am asking you again…Did you scratch around in my room and in my cupboards?" Again I pleaded innocence. She beat me up with a belt, and it was brutal. I did not cry during those beatings. She said she would stop beating me if I told her the truth. But I continued to profess my blamelessness. When she got tired of beating me, she told me to go outside and think about what I needed to tell her.

I went outside to think and called out for Evy next door. She and Luthi came over and I asked them what to do. Luthi's eyes flamed with an anger I had not seen before and he begged me to tell her that I knew she had taken the shoes. But I had thought through my options, and telling her the truth was not one of them. I knew that she was not finished with me and I braced myself for the next round of torture. But no one, not even Evy, could have prepared a little girl for what was to come.

I was sitting on the bench near the outside washing area, where I would normally wash the dog's blankets, and I did not hear her coming. I heard an unfamiliar sound and felt a burning on my head simultaneously. Before I could react I heard and felt those same sensations again and again. I turned around and managed to see the board that she was beating me with. There were thick, long nails protruding out of a wooden board and she lifted it again and brought it down with an implausible weight and force on my head. I remember seeing pure evil and hatred in her eyes before that board hit my head. I knew I was not crying but my eyes were filling with what I thought were tears, until I saw those red drops dripping on the floor. The red tears transformed themselves from tiny droplets into heavy drops and eventually into a steady flow. I was bleeding profusely and could not see much after that. But I did not see, hear or feel much after that, except the music of Shirley Bassey getting louder and louder until there was no place where her voice did not exist.

"I am what I am, I am my own very special kind of person, I beat my own drum, some say it's foolish, I say it's pretty...It's my world and I don't give a damn about lost emotions...My world so why not look at things from a different angle...Your life is a mess, till you can say, hey world...I am what I am."

I have no idea why that particular song came to my mind, when there were so many songs that I knew. At some point it felt that I would surely die, as I had never seen so much blood. Perhaps I should have been singing a hymn, like *Amazing Grace* or better still, *In the Sweet By and By, We shall Meet on that Beautiful Shore* to help usher me to the right side of the other world. But it was the beautiful, powerful and almost defiant sounds of that voice that echoed through my mind that day.

But I stopped hearing Ms Shirley's song when I became aware of something tugging at my head. I realised that I was with Doctor Fixit, the one who was treating me for my laziness. I did not know how I got there but lay still not making a sound. All my attention was now on the needle that was going in and out of my head. The doctor was fixing me once again, darning my broken head like an over-worn and tired sock. I received quite a few stitches but never cried or felt any pain or fear in that moment.

A few days after that, I was recovering on doctor's orders in the house alone when everyone had left for the day to school and work. My head was bandaged and

I wore a brace of some sort over my head. Vena snuck into the house to visit me. We discussed creating a theatrical comedy show with a fictional character that gets broken down and put together with a magical needle and thread, who has a problem of laziness but could be cured by weekly shots from Doctor Fixit. Although my head was painful, I laughed so much that day. Vena always made me laugh. I was tired when he left.

This was not a time of reporting human rights abuses, neither did I have a single adult in this world who would believe me if I told them the atrocities that were being committed against me, or who cared enough to ask about the sadness and aloofness reflected in my eyes. People always commented that I liked to keep to myself, though, and told me I was very unsociable. I once tried to tell my father but his response silenced me for a long time. It was Luthi's idea that I tell him that I was not happy there and I later told him not to give me advice, ever again.

But the missing shoe incident was to be a turning point. When my father fetched us for the holidays, I managed to conceal the shoes in my suitcase. Cruella made the mistake of telling my father about what a "raw and uncouth" child I was, and that I could not take care of my belongings, including my shoes that I had lost. My father told her that he would deal with me at home. When we were getting into the car my father was very vocal about how he was going to deal with me for being an embarrassment to him.

I do not know what made me speak at that point, because I had learnt from an early age to keep quiet, especially when the injustice was directed at me. Perhaps it was that I had had enough. I had been beaten down and stitched up for a crime I did not commit, and I could not be beaten up again for the same crime.

Perhaps it was also hearing Luthi's words ringing in my head imploring me to, then I said, "Dad, I did not lose my shoes. I have them in my suitcase. She took them and hid them in her wardrobe."

Of course my dad went on and on about how I liked to talk back to adults and about being a liar and an embarrassment to him and his mother's name. I really never liked it when my dad said that I was an embarrassment to his mother's name, because my Gogo never thought that, and I was sure that she actually liked me. And even though she had a sadness in her eyes, she never tried to make me look "less African" as other people did.

Then he said, "Where are the shoes now? If you have them, go and fetch them." I fetched the shoes from my suitcase and showed them to him. For the first time that I could really remember, my dad noticed me, and asked me if I was telling the truth. "Yes, Dad, I am telling the truth, I have been barefoot all term because she hid my shoes. She hit me for losing the shoes and I have stitches in my head."

Perhaps my own father's experience of being victimised and beaten down as a child stirred inside of him, but something came over him. He asked my sister if I was telling the truth and my sister confirmed the stories and also told him I had been in hospital. He got out of the car, asked my mother, sister and me to join him, and went back into the house. We sat in the lounge and my father scolded Cruella for what had happened. She retaliated by telling him that I will amount to nothing, that I would be pregnant and a tramp by the time I was sixteen and that I was a liar. She insisted that she did not take those shoes. She went on to tell my parents that their children will all amount to nothing, and that her children were "one hundred per cent better" than theirs. What she said did not evoke any feelings inside of me. I was subject to those insults from her and other people for years and there was nothing that she had said in that lounge on that day that she had not said before. I was, however, closely watching my father's reactions to her mutterings and observed without any emotion how he was shocked by the venom cascading like a torrent from her mouth, and how he was defending me. A part of me wondered why he had not been protecting me all along, from her, himself, and the egregiousness into which I was born.

My father asked us to fetch any items that we may have left and to pack all our belongings in the car. There was a sense of relief driving away from that house because I knew that my father would never take us back there. I was not under any illusions, even at that age, that my life would get better, but I knew that it would change. And that was comforting enough at the time…I needed a change.

But my father did not know the half of it. He did not know that her husband would visit the room where we slept at night and peer under our blankets with a torch. There is something about an adult invading the private space of little girls that is difficult to explain. There was a humiliation of someone having access to viewing a very private part of you, the fear of not knowing what he was going to do and the terror of not knowing when he was going to come into the room again.

I am not sure if there are parts of the experience that I refuse to remember. Later on in my life when I was in therapy, discussions about these incidents ended in a stalemate between the therapists and myself. I detest talking about this matter. Maybe some things are just too heinous to talk about, to anyone, even to a therapist. A few times I have tried to talk to my sister about these incidents. Once it was after we had learnt that a family member had been sexually abused, and we spoke about

Harding briefly. Our discussions of Harding are always very brief, perhaps we both don't like to discuss these matters. Mostly when I would see him enter the room, he would lift our blankets and look, and shine a torch under our blankets. Sometimes he would make muffling sounds while he was viewing. Once his hand touched my thigh and I reacted by pulling my legs closer to my chest, and then he left the room. I don't know how many times he came into the room when I was asleep but I doubt he could have done anything more, because I became a very light sleeper, a condition that thirty years later I am yet to overcome.

There was a conspiracy for sure. She would forbid us from wearing underwear when we went to bed, and conveniently her husband would come into our room to have a look. Our bedroom door also had the keys removed, so we could not lock it when we went to bed. She was not responsible for any cleaning in that house, but there were times when my sister and I would be very embarrassed to watch her stand on a chair, wearing a very short shirt-dress, and then reach up to dust the areas of the wall that were closest to the ceiling. When she did this, her buttocks and vaginal area would be fully exposed, and this would be emphasised when she bent down deliberately to fetch something from the floor. She seemed to do this ritual either when my sister and I were in a position where we could not avoid the view, and when her husband was around. As a child I never understood why she so freely exposed her genitals in that way. Especially when I would have done anything to prevent that man from entering our room.

There was a period, I am not sure how long it lasted, that he did not come into our room. He was very sick and in bed for some time and everyone seemed to be very, very worried and concerned about the state of his health.

The power that this man and woman had over our lives in those years was immense; she knew it and she exploited it to the maximum. My mother not only always made sure that our suitcases were packed with clothes that were fashionable at the time, but also that we had enough of everything. My sister and I were hardly to use those dresses. They would make the long journey with us to Harding, and inevitably make the long journey back with us without being worn. She saw no need for us to be fancy. We were so far away from home and there was no appeal process to all and any of her intractable decisions. I did not know it at the time, but later I got to understand that some of her actions were based on a jealousy. Although my friend Luthi often said that she was a jealous woman, I never really knew then what that meant.

This was the 1970s and many people of colour were not people of superfluous means. Apartheid was in full swing and the teaching profession was a way out for many people of colour. The income through teaching was enough not to starve, but there were no spare funds to go on holidays, buy fancy clothes or own fancy cars like my father did. It was a standard existence where average was the order of the day. But we came from a home where nothing was average. We had a large house and a large property, our lives were expansive and there were always people living with us, visiting us and my father was always helping other people. As a result, even people in my father's sphere became people of means. I figured later that Cruella's agreeing to take us on as boarders must have been an economic driven decision, because my father would pay her monthly for the cost of keeping us there. But there was a jealousy, the more I come to think about it. Many of her insults were of a comparative type, so she would talk about how bad I was in relation to her, her family or her children. Cruella must have had very bad things happen to her in her life to turn out the way she did. Perhaps it was also very difficult for her to reconcile her fair skin with her average life.

And I guess that would explain her motivations for her decision in one of the years that we stayed with her. I have never struggled at school, and because I started school earlier than most children, I found myself in the same grade as my sister, because she had had to repeat a grade earlier on. Cruella was our class teacher the year I found myself in the same grade as my sister and Cruella's daughter, who was three years older than I was. Despite my age, I was a top ten student, and even in those early years I knew that I should do well enough to avoid beatings, but not well enough to be the top student...that would attract too much attention, after all, who was I to dare to be at the top? That was not the script that many people around me saw for me. She thus had no justification for insults in relation to my academic ability, and I made sure that my school work was always in order and on time. But she was the one with the power, and she used it, even against my academic proficiency. At the end of that year, my report card read "TOO YOUNG AND IMMATURE TO PROCEED TO THE NEXT GRADE". A well above average student to repeat a grade, can you imagine the boredom that I had to endure the following year? But I was powerless, no adult fighting for my rights, no appeals process. It was final.

The year I repeated the grade, she was my teacher once again, but that was the last time I would be subject to her whims, hatred and bitterness. But that was also a very sad year for South Africa. Steve Biko, a great leader of this country and an inspiration to many black

63

people, was arrested and interrogated in Police Room 619 in Port Elizabeth. He was clubbed and tortured for over twenty hours, resulting in serious brain injuries. The police put him in the back of a police van close to death, naked and shackled and drove for over one thousand kilometres to Pretoria. He died the following day in police custody. No one was ever brought to justice for this.

After we left Harding, my father eventually learnt of the man's excursions to our bedroom through my sister's recounting of events to my mother. He reacted by taking us for virginity testing and that would become an added feature of my life. I hated going for those very invasive tests. It seemed to me that nothing was private. I longed to be alone and have the privacy I so very desperately wanted. Sometimes silence is the best action.

Pencils were not just for writing

I entered the next grade in a new school. The school was perched on the rolling hills of the midlands in the Natal province. It catered for the local population, but mainly it attracted pupils from all over the country as it provided boarding facilities. I am sure that parents sent their children there because it was a boarding school, run mainly by German nuns who were notorious for their discipline.

I was twelve years old when my sister and I were enlisted into the boarding school system of the Catholics. The school was organised on a set of rituals and schedules, some religious and some necessitated by the organisational requirements of housing so many girls and boys who had to be educated, accommodated, en-churched and cultured. The boys' dormitories were situated some distance from those of the girls, and outside of school activities, boys and girls were not to mingle at all! The classrooms, however, were co-ed, but during the breaks, the genders were separated once more. When the lunch bell rang, each gender would go back to their dormitories and dine at their respective eating halls. The school had one Olympic size swimming pool and there was a clear schedule when the boys or the girls were allowed to swim.

I could not swim then, but all boarders were required to swim. The school did not have swimming coaches as such, but the teachers who could swim would attempt to teach students when they were on supervision duty at the pool. There was a fearlessness about me at the time. I got into the pool a few times in the shallow end and loved the feeling of the water, but I didn't like being among those in the shallow end and envied those girls who were diving in at the deep-end and doing laps across the length and width of the pool. Spurred on by the need to conquer the deep end, I went to sit at the edge of the diving board area with my legs dangling into the water, and contemplated what could happen if I just jumped in. At first I felt quite brave about the thought of doing that, then I got scared. I stood up to move away from the deep end, and at that moment a girl was passing by and we made contact. I do not know if I lost balance and fell into the pool or if she pushed me. Perhaps it was my strong desire to conquer the deep end that, if she had not pushed me, probably would have caused me to trip over my own feet and fall in.

That experience perhaps solidified the fear, survival and conquering spirit in me. I had a strong desire to swim, I had fear about what could happen to me, I fell in or was pushed, I was forced to struggle and find my way up, then I mastered the art of swimming. I do not remember how long I struggled, trying to get afloat and stay afloat, what I choose to remember is how it felt when I started floating. It felt good. After that incident my swimming ability and prowess improved exponentially every time I entered the pool. I had many fun hours in that pool for the six years that I attended that boarding school.

I also spent many hours in the detention process at this school. The year I spent repeating a grade that had provided no academic challenge for me in the first take must have changed me somehow. I was a model pupil up until that point, I did my work diligently, and on time and I rarely made any waves inside and outside the classroom. But that repeat year saw me going to the headmaster's office often for ill discipline, including passing notes around the classroom and making a noise in the hallways, or deliberately stepping out of line in the assembly points. I cannot pinpoint why I started becoming naughty. Perhaps it had to do with boredom of going over work that didn't challenge me at all, perhaps it had to do with the feeling of powerlessness in a system where other people decided my fate on whims. Perhaps it had to do with the realisation that hard work did not really pay off; it did not really matter.

The feeling that you cannot do anything to change things for the better is oppressive to your soul. Perhaps I realised that if I could not change things for the better in that instance, I could change them for the worse.

There was a kind of logic in that, if indeed that was the motivation for my conscious and subconscious acts of defiance. If you were beaten up, humiliated and abused for doing nothing bad, at least do something to justify the reactions. If you are naughty you suffer the consequences. Perhaps we all are in search of a kind of logic, where action deserves a reaction, a just and equitable reaction.

By the time I got to the boarding school, that logic had perhaps taken root in me. The detention took various forms. You could be punished by being asked to clean the public school toilets for a week, cleaning the rhubarb gardens near the dining hall, or assisting the librarian with packing of books. Really? That was punishment? Did these people know what and where I had come from? Those punishments were like picnics for me. Cleaning, cooking, scrubbing was second nature to me. It was daily duties in Harding and when we were at my parents' house for holiday breaks I would engage in these activities because my father believed in not spoiling children and, more specifically, that girls should do these things. From a very tender age I could cook, bake, clean, wash and iron for a family of ten people, with no sweat. By the time I came to this school, I could drive a car and I could operate a cash register and "run" the business for my mother in her absence. I could also count stacks of money and do banking for my father's businesses. Cleaning toilets? Helping to pack the library? Punishment! Really?

But South Africa was divided along racial lines, and this school was no exception. Black people stayed in black areas and went to black schools; and white people stayed in white areas and went to white-only schools. Indian people stayed in Indian areas and went to Indian schools. In between those clearly defined races, there existed a group of people who were put together by the apartheid government in a racial group, and they called these people "Coloured". They proceeded to create areas where Coloured people would reside and go to school. Coloured people were mixed race. Anyone who was mixed, whether Caucasian and African, African and Chinese, mixed race and Caucasian, or Indian and Caucasian, were classified as Coloured. Nowhere in the world does this classification exist legally as a distinct racial group but in South Africa.

Within the Coloured group, there was also further classification. There was the "Cape Coloured" classification, which mainly referred to mixed people from the Cape area, and the mixture was mainly between Malay and Xhosa people, or Malay and the Xhoisan people, who are the indigenous or first people of South Africa. Then there was the "Other Coloured" classification, which referred to all other mixed race people, mainly between African and other race groups.

This was the late 1970s and the official racial classification system of the apartheid policy was entrenched in South African society. Although apartheid as a policy began officially in 1948 when Dr DF Malan, the prime architect of the policy, led the National Party into office, racial segregation was practised since the 1700s when Dutch colonisers established laws that separated white settlers and native Africans. These practices continued after the British occupation in 1795 and led to the placing of Africans into specific areas that would later, in the 1970s, be called Bantustans or Homelands. By the time of the formation of the Union of South Africa in 1910, when the Boer Republics united with Britain, there were around three hundred reserves for native Africans in the country.

The Nationalist Party began to institute a number of policies that sought to "ensure the survival of the white race" and to keep the different races separate on every level of society and in every facet of life. They started with laws that prohibited both sexual intercourse and marriages between white and black people. Then came the Population Registration Act in 1950, which categorised every South African by race, and required people to carry with them at all times their racial identification books. If you were caught without this reference book, you would be fined or imprisoned. In this year too they would pass the Group Areas Act, which was really the core foundation of the apartheid system. It provided for allocation of land for different race groups and made it illegal for people to live outside of these areas. Far too many black people were violently uprooted from their homes and moved into reserves or areas in the cities reserved for their race group. Because black labour would be needed in these white-only areas, separate transportation and other amenities were created for them.

In order for this system to work effectively there needed to be a robust classification system that separated the races. White settlers had been in the country since 1652 and the lines between black and white were not always clear cut because Caucasian men

69

had been having intercourse, voluntarily or not, with African women for a long time already. I suppose this is why the apartheid government's first laws were about prohibiting sexual intercourse between whites and blacks. This presented a dilemma for the classification process though. Some very humiliating practices were employed to separate "white" from "other".

One of these was the pencil test. It involved sliding a pencil into your hair if your race was uncertain. If the pencil fell to the floor, you would pass the test and be considered white. There are many Afrikaner "white" people who are darker than my mother's family, because although many passed the pencil test, where the hair type was the decider, their African blood would show in their skin tones. There are many very sad stories in South Africa of two "white" people who give birth to a child that looks like me, and these children and their parents have been ostracised from the "white" population. These children probably feel the way I do when I walk down the street with my mother. Or how my father felt when he had to drive the car and my mother would have to sit at the back of the car to avoid the problems that they normally encountered, very much like Morgan Freeman was driving Miss Daisy, except that this was his wife, and mother of his children.

Later on in my life, in post-apartheid South Africa, I would have the experience of meeting my white Personal Assistant's husband. When I looked at him I realised that he was actually mixed race even though he was classified white. One of the people in the organisation made a comment to her that her babies could come out black and her response scared and surprised me to some degree. She said "If he lied to me about being white, I will divorce him!" She ran into the toilet and cried for a while. When she returned she was calm and seem pleased when she told me that she had nothing to worry about because she had called her husband and he assured her that he was a regular white guy. That is how absurd the classification system was and how much currency it actually did carry.

If the pencil, however, was stuck in your hair and did not fall to the ground, you would fail the test and be classified Coloured. If my father had taken my sister for this test, she would have been classified white. My father and I would never have passed that test.

There was a variation of this test, though. if you had been classified black, and wished to be reclassified Coloured, the pencil would be placed in your hair, and you would be asked to shake your head. If the pencil fell out of your hair when you shook it, you would be reclassified Coloured, but if it stayed in place, you would remain black.

My paternal grandmother, after whom I was named, was to be subjected to reclassification. She was classified black African, as she was indeed black, and was required to carry a reference book. Her husband, her step sister who was his first wife, and all her children were classified Coloured. When things became intolerable for her in her home, my father decided to move her away from that area, and bought a house for her which he had to register in his name, because she was not allowed to own a house or live in the Coloured area. My grandmother, in order to live with her children, had to be reclassified.

I remember those times vividly. My aunts "hot combed" her hair. This process involved heating an iron comb on a stove, and then combing the hair through until it was straightened. My grandmother had long natural hair at the time, and after they had done the hot combing process, it was even longer because the natural curl had been straightened out. She looked very different from the grandmother I knew growing up. She used to braid her natural hair, mainly by parting it in the middle and making two braids on each side. But mostly, as per her culture and traditions, she would put her hair in a scarf. Hair really does define one's appearance and if you change it, your appearance changes significantly. My grandmother was taken to the Homeland department, and undertook the pencil test. She passed the test, was reclassified Coloured, and was able to live in the house that my father had bought for her.

Perhaps this is where the culture of straightening of hair was born and solidified in the people classified as Coloured.

My grandmother did not need to change her surname because she had my grandfather's surname through marriage, which he in turn got from his father, who was English. But for many other black people who tried to get reclassified, they would have to change their surnames. "Ndlovu" for example is a surname among black people in South Africa, which means "elephant". During the reclassification process, many with that surname would become Oliphant or Olifant, which was the Afrikaans translation of "elephant". My grandmother's family, her brothers and children, did not apply for reclassification and kept their surname, which was Nkosi.

Many African people applied to be reclassified because although you would still not be regarded as a first class citizen, you would be afforded a few more privileges than if you were classified black. Many of these black people applying for reclassification would often learn Afrikaans, which was the main language of the Afrikaner people, to aid the process of reclassification. The best analogy I could use to describe this system is that it is like being in a prison but Coloured people had been given the right to work in the prison kitchen by their warders. They were still prisoners like black people, but within the prison they were afforded some privileges. It was absurd!

This system differed significantly from the United States of America classification of black people where "one drop of African blood" was enough to make one black. A friend of mine from Cameroon with whom in my mid thirties I had many debates about race has specific issues with this classification system, however, stating that white people want to keep their race pure, but do not mind that the black African race is getting diluted. I told him that if both races wanted to remain pure, they needed to stop going across the racial line to make babies!

Among all these Coloured people, there also existed an unofficial classification based on the hue of the skin tone and the hair type. The more African the hair and the darker the complexion tone, the more difficult life was for you. Fair skin and silkier hair generally meant an easier life within that grouping. But not outside of it. At the end of the day if you were not classified white or Caucasian, you were disenfranchised.

In this boarding school I got to meet both classifications of Coloured people, and I got to witness and experience the unofficial classification process too. We were supposed to be "Other Coloured", by virtue of the Swazi, English, Chopi and Irish heritage of my parents – the mix was Nguni and Caucasian. But the official classification of the Coloured people did not really mean much among that group; what mattered most was what you looked like. I would have occupied the lowest rung of that unofficial classification by virtue of my dark skin and African hair, and my sister would have occupied the upper echelons based on her silky hair, fair skin and green eyes.

Although I had known from an early age I was different, the currency of those differences only played out significantly when we visited my mother's family, in the four years I lived with them or during school holidays, and somewhat in my previous schooling. In my hometown the term used to describe black women was "scons" and parents would warn their male children about sleeping with "scons". And to this date when people from this Coloured group notice something worthwhile in a black African or a person with a dark skin they will make statements like,

"He is dark, but he has a brain."

"She is very dark but at least she has a good heart."

"Shame she married a black guy, but he has money."

"He is now with a black girl, but shame she loves him and will do anything for him."

"Oh, do you know that Jessica is dating that black actor, but his father is a big guy, hey!"

The one that really brings out the Vena in me is "Why is he making dreadlocks, because he really has nice hair", as if dreadlocks are for people who have bad hair. Somehow, somewhere there must have been a convention where people discussed, debated, caucused, agreed, resolved and gazetted that Caucasian hair was good and African hair was bad. But the worst of it is that these things, even today, are said in my presence. This is the reason I do not like to visit people who talk this way and I avoid them because listening to this stuff and not saying anything makes them think that you agree with them. It makes you an accomplice to the inanity. And the reality is you cannot spend your leisure time trying to set people straight about their asinine beliefs. And besides, can you ever have stimulating conversations with people who think like this?

I have met many fair skinned people in this group who are very different. In fact sometimes it is people who look just like me that discriminate the most. When I was younger I could not really understand this, but later I was to understand this phenomenon better. I guess when you turn out dark in this community, you can either have a "so what" attitude and be "black and proud" or you can try to be "more Coloured" or "more white" so that you can fit into the community that you live in. And this is a very understandable need, because you want to feel cared for, accepted and feel a sense of belonging. It is a universal need of mankind as a whole. If you gravitate towards the latter, then it is perhaps necessary that you do not associate with people who look too much like you because they are a visual reminder of that which you do not accept about yourself. So you call them names as a way of showing that you are different. Sometimes the darker skinned people marry fair-skinned people so that their children are not a constant reminder of their own blackness. But genetics has a way of catching up, and sometimes a child that looks like me comes along, who has to carry the brunt.

Many times Coloured people would pray that their sons and daughters will not marry or have children with Africans. Imagine that? They would actually ask God that He will keep his own creation away from someone's son or daughter. It is very difficult to take advice from these people when they tell you that you need to go to church more and read your bible more. And it is these people who are the ones that say "When will these blacks stop using the race card?" Well, maybe when you stop using it! And maybe when race and colour does not carry as much currency as it does now. So do you see why whiteness, on its own, has never impressed me? While I can understand why people become this way, as a means of surviving and fitting in, none of this stuff can ever be described as intelligent, smart or wise.

Mostly when they say these phrases they don't even realise how racist those statements are. Because when they encounter the very rampant racism from white people against them that is still very prevalent in South African society even in 2013, you hear them complaining and crying foul about racism. *"The most potent weapon in the hands of the oppressor is the mind of the oppressed."* How very right Steve Biko was.

In South Africa this phenomenon of discriminating against your own is not reserved for this group of people. Among the Indian population in South Africa I have seen it play out many times. First the discrimination is directed towards African people. If you grew up or schooled in the Kwa-Zulu Natal province where the highest percentage of the Indian population live, you will have no doubt witnessed how some Indian people treat Africans. It is not a nice thing to see.

On the way back from school, my father would normally stop in Durban for lunch. My mother liked curries, and there was a restaurant near the Blue Lagoon where we would often eat. One day my father lost his temper with the Indian shop owner when he saw how he treated his African workers, and the derogatory racial terms used to describe them. I have often witnessed them using profanities and racial slurs against Africans, often accompanied by a slap on the back of the head. The incidents were far from isolated.

This racism against Africans among some in this population group is still prevalent today. I guess people cannot just change what they feel because of a change of government; these things are ingrained, with a generational grip so tight. For sure you stand a much better chance of taking a white man or woman home to introduce to your family than an African person. I have had many Indian friends over my lifetime and when we discuss the discrimination among the Coloured group, they will readily tell you stories of the same phenomenon in their own community, that they have been subjected to. I have seen the fear and/or refusal of some Indian women to introduce their African lovers to other Indian people. However, if it is a white guy, the person is not just introduced but promoted within their families and the community at large. In both the study and work areas of my life, I would notice how "progressive" people from this racial group struggle with racism within themselves. I figure that before one can get rid of discrimination and racism in the world, you have to deal with it within yourself. It is difficult to hate that which you see in another, if you love that in yourself.

But later I would learn that this discrimination was not against African people alone, but against their own as well. It appears to be much better if you are fairer in the Indian population too. Cosmetic companies have made billions of dollars on "get white and beautiful" products, the same way that the companies who provide weaves or chemicals for black hair are doing very well, even when the global economy is in a state of decline. Advertisements to promote these products show a dark skinned actor feeling bad about himself; a Bollywood star then shows him the secret of his own stardom. The dark skinned man gets lighter as he uses the creams and soon his life improves and he feels better about himself. Bollywood actors like Shahid Kapoor and Shahrukh Khan promote these skin whitening products. Many of these products have harmful ingredients, so when I saw this statement from Sorisha Naidoo, who markets these products, I was really concerned for the health of future generations:

"I have clients who put their children on the product – some as young as nine years old, with a reference from dermatologists, so that they are not the slightly darker child in school or in the class picture. In parts of the Indian community, being the slightly darker cousin or sister means that no matter how striking, intelligent or skilled you are, being fair still means more."

In the African continent as a whole researchers revealed the following prevalence of skin lightening use: 25% prevalence in Bamako, 52% in Dakar, 35% in Pretoria and 77% in Lagos. That means seventy seven out of every one hundred people who live in Lagos try to make their skins whiter. The study, reported on in *Science in Africa*, states that even in modern times the majority of black men prefer light-skinned women as partners, girlfriends and wives, and that light skinned women are perceived as 'attractive, intelligent, moral, sexually more desirable, even chaste'; whereas dark-skinned women are regarded as 'mean, evil, stupid, even not trust-worthy'.

What I know from my own experience growing up in a mixed race home is that when you are a black woman, all the cues around you point to your being less than, not good enough. Even some black men who shout out against racism and write about it are part of the statistics that reflect the preference for fair skinned women. You grow up knowing that there is something not okay with you, and it starts in your own home. So it is not surprising, although very sad to me, that many black women use skin lighteners, straighten their hair and wear weaves. Sometimes people just want to fit in and belong. It is one of the greatest needs of human kind; to fit in, belong and to identify with. When you choose not to follow this path, it is a lonely path to travel, a lonely place to reside in. But it is also the place where you feel best about yourself. The time of Steve Biko was never over.

The reality too is that those who turned out light skinned did not request to be born that way, it just happened that way. They were born into a world where light skin means *better than*, as reflected in the various research. Yes, some of these women exploit this and make women who are dark skinned feel that there is something wrong with them, but many do not. These women have another challenge, because amongst dark-skin black women they are not readily accepted, they are made to feel that they created the social favour into which they were born. But the reality is that they did not, so they too have identity issues, wondering where it is that they belong. They certainly do not belong and fit in among the white population, in fact they are rejected there too.

The previous school in Harding was also reserved for the Coloured group of people. Some of the beatings I got from Cruella were often accompanied by references to my skin colour and I was aware of some of the teachers' remarks regarding complexion. A white teacher once marked my work very low when I felt I had done a lot better than the mark she gave me reflected. I complained to a family member and she responded "Just keep quiet, don't say anything, you are the dark one." I wonder just how many people like me were treated very badly and no one will ever get to know what they endured because they were "the dark one". But my awareness of these skin hue differences did not match the torture and humiliation of the regime under which I lived at the time. It was only when I got to the boarding school that these issues presented themselves crudely and openly and I was to be "free" to witness them. In these spaces brothers would deny their sisters, and sisters would deny their brothers if they looked anything like me.

In this obtuse form of classification, ideally, the higher you are on the ladder, white and silky, the more intelligent, smarter, and faster you should be. Right? After all was it not predicated on an ideology that the white race is the master race and superior in every form?

This ideology, Nordicism, was founded on the basis that Nordic people were a superior race, a master race, and they considered all non-Nordic people to be inferior. The belief was in the superiority of the white race, especially in the areas of culture and intelligence. The Jews, Gypsies, black people, brown people, yellow people and mixed race people were considered sub human – the *Untermensch*, as Germany's Hitler would define the non-Nordics. His own obsession to cleanse Germany of the pollutant races through his eugenics programme to preserve the Aryan, master race was founded on this philosophy. He argued that the highest civilisation and culture are found among these races, and that even where there is advanced civilisation and culture to be found among the non-Nordic areas, it is the fairer skinned people that display more intelligence and who are really responsible for advancement. I guess he had never heard of Hannibal of Carthage, with his brilliant and trail blazing military strategy that marched into Capua, noble and triumphant. A strategy that the Roman Empire and others would later emulate. Although Hitler refused to shake Jesse Owens' hand after he made history and broke records by winning four gold medals in the 1936 Olympics, this would put his beliefs in a tailspin, and Albert Speer would later relate Hitler's sentiments about Owens,

"Each of the German victories, and there were a surprising number of these, made him happy, but he was highly annoyed by the series of triumphs by the marvellous coloured American runner, Jesse Owens. People whose antecedents came from the jungle were primitive, Hitler said with a shrug; their physiques were stronger than those of civilised whites and hence should be excluded from future games."

According to this philosophy, the top honours in this school I was attending, in academia and cultural pursuits, should be dominated by the white and silky. But this was most certainly not the case and this was an observation I had made from an early age in my life in my own home. My father, a black man, was the leader of the pack. I figured he must have had intelligence to build an empire for himself without the support of family, and within the very difficult conditions that apartheid created for black people. And none of my mother's family or the other white people they had married could compete, even though they had privilege bestowed on them. I even considered that their fear of my skin colour rubbing off on them a form of lower intelligence. Vena and I often made jokes about this stupidity. I was the "dark one", but I began school at age four and could out-read anyone. Although the white and silky might be revered as "beautiful" and get the benefit of the doubt from parents and teachers, when it came to something you can do something about, and the brain, they were not different.

In fact, I noticed that those who looked like me did better, and not because they were necessarily cleverer, but they were smarter because they used their talents and circumstances to strive for something better. Perhaps when you have unwarranted favour, because of something as inconsequential as eye colour, you don't have to apply yourself as much. Things come easier, so you do not have to fight and struggle to achieve, you just have favour, for something that you did not work for or create yourself. Of course these are all generalisations, but they are my observations. As a result I have never felt in awe of fairness on its own. The ONLY place where they had one on me was that their skin colour brought them privilege and favour. That I could do nothing about.

The worst form of abuse and discrimination I faced in my life has come from this group of people, and all the ugliness of the sub culture of racism. Personally I do not refer to myself as a Coloured, but rather as an African or black woman. One day when there is no currency behind race and gender, I would like to refer to myself as a person. But I know that day will not come in my lifetime nor in that of my children, or their children's children. Race and gender have significant currency not only in this country; throughout my travels around the world, I have seen that they indeed have global currency.

One just has to look at racism in a sport as universal as football or soccer, and the refusal of those who really have the power to do something substantial and consequential to change things. Sepp Blatter's comments about Kevin-Prince Boateng "running away" when he left the pitch after racist remarks were made by football fans and his suggesting that the club must forfeit the match is a typical response from those who have not been a victim of racial and or gender abuse. But his denial that racism in football was not an issue and his claims that any race-related incidents that occurred during the game could be solved by a handshake at the final whistle set my internal torrent abuzz, and I start to feel that volcanic pressure from deep within me. It reminds me of my own circumstances when family members who do not experience this abuse, or people who do not know what it is to grow up under a system that dehumanises you, tell you to "just get over it". How much I wish that a handshake could erase it all. I would have shaken a million hands in my life time. It is indeed sad that one of the most powerful men on the planet cannot use that power to change things for the better.

How history will judge you, Sepp Blatter, is not whether you had power, but what you did with that power when you had it. Did you use it to change things for the better? Were you able to use it to really change things that are difficult to change? Thank you Kevin-Prince Boateng for using your power to take a stand, even though you were not sure what the consequence of that action would be to you personally.

The other characteristic of my abusers has been their religion. I have noticed that the people who have treated me with contempt and who have displayed the cruellest forms of discrimination against me have all with equal force told me and others how wonderful God was, and that he loved me. My readings into oppressive regimes around the world show an uneasy relationship between religion and oppression.

Apartheid was carried out with bible in hand, the missionaries accompanied colonisers around Africa, and the United States of America was founded on slavery, near extinction of indigenous people and the bible. I have never taken easily to organised forms of religion. I pray every day, all the time, and I have a relationship with God that transcends any form that organised religions can take, or the people who look down on me with a condescendence in their eyes and a bible on their lips. I am also not ignorant of the fact that Catholicism was used substantially to justify and promote the African slave trade. Africans, sub human, were meant to be oppressed because they were descendants of Ham, whose son was cursed by Noah.

Religions I have seen over my life time have been used to oppress people, particularly women, and to keep them oppressed. Judaism, Christianity and Islam all treat women as inferior to men. Women are frequently denied leadership roles, expected to be submissive and to "know" their place in the family and in society. Other religions also account for sexist beliefs and in a study on this matter, Seguino concluded that *religiousity is indeed strongly linked to gender inequalitable beliefs*, but did not find that any one religious group stood out as having more sexist attitudes than any other.

The Mormon religion puts a great deal of importance on skin colour – the godly are fair and wholesome and the disobedient are given dark skins as a curse. But when the dark skins repent, their skin becomes fair again. Hinduism has an inbred racist element and I have never been able to reconcile the amount of effort Ghandi put into promoting human rights for Indians in South Africa with his spending significantly less time in changing the absolutely worst form of dehumanisation I have witnessed in my life – that against the Dalit people in his own country. Although at some point later in his life he made some effort to speak up for their rights, he had also refused to support the Dalits in their own campaign to be allowed to pray in temples. Over one hundred and sixty million people, almost four times the population of South Africa, are, according to a belief system, subject to the most horrendous form of existence. I would be moved when reading about their plight, but when I got to engage directly with this phenomenon later in my life, I was to become physically ill for weeks. It is very difficult to eat or sleep at night after you have witnessed the plight of the Dalit people. On reflection, when Ghandi agreed with the British that the white population was indeed the predominant race in an African country, his fight to ensure that Indians should be classified higher than indigenous Africans, and his pleas to the British to allow Indians to fight alongside them, against the Zulu, was not really out of sync with the caste system beliefs that he held. After the British allowed him to join their fight against the Zulu nation, Ghandi himself led a small corps of volunteers to stretcher and treat wounded British soldiers in the war. I am sure that in that he must have seen the folly of his stance and the impact of the internalised oppression of which he was a product.

There is much to celebrate about Ghandi. He made the most notable individual effort on self discipline, which many of us could learn from, especially me. He was committed to getting independence from the British for India, and he strived to live in a manner that this and other generations can learn from. For sure we would not have the dangers of global warming looming over us if we all followed his way of life, particularly this generation, being too focused on excessive consumerism and materialism. He is a shining example of what mankind can do when they have such strong convictions. He campaigned tirelessly for the elevation of women's standing in society, something that few male or female leaders can boast of. He has an enormous place in history, which can never be denied.

But perhaps this really makes me understand how powerful religion can be, that even such a formidable man, a great thinker, prolific writer and committed activist for the human rights of Indians, can refuse to support the Dalits' rights to pray in temples, and volunteer to actively support the British army against indigenous Africans in the land of their birth, and agree with the British that not only was the white race predominant, but that Africans were the lowest on the rung.

Later on in my life I would actively participate in the World Conference Against Racism, and discover how prevalent racism has been in various religions around the world, and how religions can perpetuate prejudice. The spokesperson of the World Council of Churches made reference to how indigenous Maori people were excluded by the missionaries when they formed the Church of England in New Zealand, because they believed there was a difference between Europeans and Maoris.

Towards the end of the conference, Cardinal Wilfred Napier said, "So many people have had bad experiences of racism, which they probably haven't dealt with. We have become conscious that you can't just expect it to fade away. Some of it has to be brought to the surface and dealt with specifically." I appreciated his response to racism and Christianity because so often victims of racism are expected to "just get over it", although later I would not share his views about how to deal with paedophilia within the church. Institutions, like churches, the police force, places of work and schools, are microcosms of the society we live in, and if you experience and/or practise discrimination in your home, you will experience it and/or practice it in your churches and your schools.

Many religious leaders have fought against racism and oppression in South Africa, some gave their lives for this cause, and the reality that the very religions that they serve have participated in perpetuating oppression cannot in any way underplay the significant role they have made in overthrowing apartheid as a system of governance.

But sometimes issues of faith have also made me laugh, because of how easy it appears to make manipulations possible. It was customary in my home for our family to pray together. Normally it would be in the morning before everyone goes off on their business, and at night before bedtime. When my father was ready to sleep then it was time to pray. Sometimes it was long after we had fallen asleep, and my father would wake us up to do our prayers.

Everyone would go onto their knees and lean on the seat of the lounge chairs with hands folded and eyes closed. My father would call out one person to say their prayers and then the person next to them was to follow with their prayers until everyone had prayed. When there were no issues in the home, the system worked. Everyone would say their prayers then off to bed we would all go.

But when there was something brewing or something that my father was not happy with, the prayer time would take on a different dimension. He would then always start the prayers himself, and talk to God about the things that were bothering him. "God, tell me, where did I go wrong that you gave me such a lazy child? Really, she drags her feet around this house as if she is an old woman. Please, God, help her to change, dear Lord!" or when he was unhappy with my mother he could pray "Father, God in Heaven, you know this heavy burden that I am carrying. Help me to carry it well, dear Lord. My wife has got a habit of spoiling these children. I have tried everything, dear Lord, but she does not listen to me. Give me strength, dear Lord, because you alone knows what it is that I am going through."

Those prayers of his usually were very lengthy and sometimes I would fall asleep because they went on and on, and because I was tired as we would normally be taken out of our sleep to pray. If his prayer was about me, when it came to my turn to pray, then I would echo his prayers, so that he did not ask me, "Is that all you need to pray about?" So I would say, "Dear Lord, please help me to stop being so lazy and forgive me for not listening to my father."

But when there was nothing brewing in the house, my father would often fall asleep during those prayer sessions. So we learnt how to fast forward the prayers and then when it came to his turn, we would wake him up, and he would ask if everyone had prayed. "Yes, Dad," we would all say. He would say his prayer, then without incident we were all off to sleep.

But one day my father snored during our prayer sessions and we proceeded to fast forward our prayers. Then we woke him up to pray. And he prayed this prayer. "Dear Lord, I now understand what Noah felt when his own children did not cover him up. Lord, when children start to make a fool of their own father, it brings a pain to my heart, Lord. Forgive them, Father, because I know that you do not take kindly to this kind of sin!" Then we knew we were in for it; he had faked his snoring to see what we were up to!

This boarding school perched on the rolling hills of Natal that my sister and I attended was a Catholic school and I participated in all the requirements of being Catholic, even though I was not born into this denomination. The Catholic religion as I have observed and experienced it is based on a set of rules, rituals, ceremonies and things to recite. We were given a Holy

Rosary, which is a necklace of beads, within the first week of arrival. Each Holy Rosary has fifty nine beads, each bead requiring a specific prayer. First we had to pray the *Our Father* prayer, then ten *Hail Mary* prayers, and lastly a *Glory Be to the Father* prayer.

Within the church itself, there was a priest and altar boys who assisted him with performing the rituals, and then there was the stations of the cross, which reflected the various stages of each of the phases of Jesus' crucifixion. I also got to learn about Palm Sunday. This was an important time of the year at our school. We had to collect palm branches and lay them on the path to the church. It is a ceremony to celebrate the entry of Jesus into Jerusalem the week before his death, and it marks the beginning of Holy Week, which ends on Easter Sunday. The girls would all dress in white and carry palm branches and recite scripts from the New Testament, directed by the priest and the nuns, who would lead the procession. Then there was a part of the church premises where the statue of Mary was kept that would be decorated with colourful stones and flowers. The school looked beautiful in these days, and it was rewarding to have participated in decorating it in those ways which I was not familiar with.

Then there was confession time, in which you could confess your sins to the priest, do the required penance and be worthy of taking communion at church. I went to my first confession and was not sure what to say, but in the end I confessed to being lazy and being naughty at school. My first penance was to say twenty *Hail Mary*s, which I recited in the church building before I went back to the dormitories.

The Catholic churches and schools have beautiful places of worship with grand architecture and attractive stained glass windows, and this school was no exception.

I was reading many books at an early age and those journeys into the worlds that those books provided me always gave me a sense of knowing about the people that I encountered. I never really took the damnation and purgatory threats very seriously and neither did I revere the priests and nuns very much. They provided no moral high ground to which I would aspire, lean on and look for spiritual guidance. I do not know why, but I never really felt that the Pope was the leader of the world spiritually. Perhaps it was those encyclopaedias I read at my parents' home. I read about the history of the Catholic Church, the corruption and the wars, and most times I did not find God or spirit in what I read. This did not make me right, I guess it's just how I felt at the time. But there is a part of me that feels that humanity has a habit of accepting something because so many people believe in it, or because so many people do it, or because so many people say it is all right, even though that something might be wrong. After all was I not a descendant of Ham?

We did church activities everyday and I enjoyed going to church, especially for the singing and because it was something different to do from the boarding school routine. I would see the bitterness in the eyes of many of the Germanic nuns in the school and they would only reflect what I had seen in my life before. As a result I feared none of them. I knew what they were capable of and I never once felt that they could do or say anything to me that I had not encountered before, or that could surprise me. Mostly I never felt that anyone could enter my thoughts. The only people who really knew me and what I thought and felt about many things were my friends Evy, Luthi and Vena. That I really did thank God for.

This feeling and my growing sense of defiance got me into much trouble. I would accompany girls who would break into the kitchen and smear peanut butter on the walls, and I would join in many excursions to the orchards at night, where we would play, make lots of noises and eat oranges until we were ready to go back to the dormitories to sleep. Sometimes the nuns would find out and we would be punished: the usual – cleaning toilets and silent treatment. I got to clean a lot of toilets in my six years at the school, which I never minded. What I did mind was the silent treatment sessions, which would involve sitting quietly and not being allowed to talk. You were not allowed to respond to anything verbally and neither was anyone supposed to talk to you. I found it difficult to reconcile my love for being alone with my dislike of silence treatment. I guess perhaps because the silent treatment was not a choice. But even this could not compare to the beatings at home or the torture I had endured before.

Although boys and girls were not allowed to mix outside of classroom activities, there was much mixing happening wherever and whenever it was possible. Many of the girls had boyfriends, and in that context, boyfriends were people you would write notes and letters to, meet behind the swimming pool area, where there were many pine trees to conceal any improper behaviours, and sometimes they would sneak out of their respective dormitories and meet at night. I had no boyfriends and had very little time for boys, except as friends to discuss and be naughty with. I had no desire or need for a boyfriend. There were two boys I remember asking me why I don't give them any attention. I did not have any plausible reason for this, but what I did know is that I had no interest in being associated with any boy in that way.

This boarding school was devoid of any political activity and discussion; we were cocooned from the realities, horrors and atrocities of the apartheid regime for those months that we were behind those walls. The only time I would be aware of the politics of the country at the time is when we went home. From the time we entered the car, my father would begin to warn us about the dangers that we could encounter. My father would take and fetch us from school at the start and end of each term, but this was to stop abruptly in the middle of the boarding school era. He would then ask his brother or send a driver to undertake the long journey, on his behalf.

The reason for this hiatus in travel with my father was directly linked to the politics of the South Africa government at the time. My father had begun to fear for his life and those of his family after he was approached by the apartheid intelligence, or Special Branch as it was called, to play an informant role for them. He was promised a myriad of benefits that could have made him a mogul, but he declined, and from then on began spending more time at home, and took on a paranoid personality. They had assured him that he had little to lose and much to gain, and that there were many people who were playing those roles, some of whom he knew very well. They also told him that they were aware of the people who were visiting his house. This put my father's life into a tailspin, and he began to be suspicious about many people who were visiting our house. One weekend a friend of my father who was living in the Eastern Transvaal province, now known as Mpumalanga, came to visit him. This was not unusual as many people had visited all the time. But that was the last time he was to visit my home. The Special Branch had sent his friend to persuade my father to work with them. My father was very surprised that his friend was working with the apartheid government, particularly because he had actively supported the cause before. After that visit my father spoke less and to fewer people. He would also learn, as I would later in my life, that "No" comes with a heavy cost to one's well being and finances, while his friend flourished.

The other reality about my home is that my father supported and provided refuge for both Frelimo freedom fighters from Mozambique and South Africans who were in exile, many of whom needed financial support and re-entry assistance into the country. As children we witnessed some leaders and foot soldiers come into our home, normally at night time. As a child I did not appreciate this, because my father would wake the girls up to prepare food and take care of the people who sought refuge. It could be any time of the night. We would have to wake up and cook food for the strangers who entered our home, and I remember vividly one night when a Frelimo soldier who was bleeding profusely came to my home for refuge, and we were tasked with preparing a bathroom, towels, and preparing food for him. On that one occasion, I delayed responding to my father's call and he responded by dragging me from my bedroom and beating me with his very large fists. We always muttered under our breaths, but knew better than to complain out loud in case my father heard us. I only got to know from my father who these people were when I was older, at university, and my father got to learn about my political activities. I also got to understand that having people in and out of our home was a decoy that worked for a long time, but no longer did. It was, I guess, time for a new strategy.

This must have been a difficult time for my father because he was a generous and gregarious man. He loved travelling and loved having many people over to his house. We were accustomed to parties that my father would host, for he loved music, people and dancing. As children we watched our father dance into the early hours of the morning with my aunts, his friends and those of my mother's. There was plenty in my home and there were always people sharing of that plenty. My father changed after that incident, he hosted fewer parties, invited fewer people over to the house and travelling almost ended altogether.

But before that travelling stopped I was to experience the brutality of my father and his intolerance of impishness from his children. During that particular school term the nuns had phoned my father to complain about my ill disciple and waywardness. I knew that the end of term would bring the wrath of my father on me. It did not moderate my behaviour for the rest of that term in any way because I knew exactly what I was in for, and doing more or less of anything would not change anything. What I did not expect was the venue for the chastisement. It was right there in the front of the school where parents would normally fetch their children at the end of term. All the girls would be sitting at the side of the main hostel building with all their suitcases, packed and ready to leave for the holidays. I saw my father pull up with the Dodge which he had imported from the USA. I smiled because I loved that car, and because I knew that no one else's parents in the school or in this country had one of those at the time. I admired how my father, a black man, could afford these luxury cars, without the benefit of his family's support and without any inheritance or back up from his own father. So it was with a smile that I ran to the car to greet my father. But the smile disappeared as quickly as it found its way to my face. "Is that what I am sending you to school for? To be phoned by the nuns and for me to hear about what you are doing here?" He beat me right there in front of all the girls. The humiliation I felt is indescribable.

I received many beatings at home too, for my report cards, although demonstrating excellence in the academic columns, always had very disturbing phrases in the remarks and comments sections. "Her behaviour leaves much to be desired, she is the most unladylike creature I have encountered in my life" is a verbatim quote from one of my report cards. My father beat me good and solid for that report card and many others like it. After these beatings I would go to visit my friends and always felt better when I was with them, especially Evy.

My sister's tattletales also accounted for many of the beatings. In those moments I hated my sister. I hated her more when my father always compared the two of us, with the comparison sessions always ending with "Why can't you be more like your sister?", which he quipped many times before, during and after those beatings. Sometimes with no provocation from my unbecoming behaviour or report cards, he would look at the way I dressed or kept my hair and comment on his desire for me to be like her. I hated both my father and sister in those moments, wondering if they could just for a while accept me as I was. I walked differently from her, I had different hair and I could never look like her. It was not the misbehaviour I wanted them to accept. I wished they would see the frightened girl inside that just wanted to be loved and accepted by a father whom she adored and admired and a sister whom she actually loved.

In truth I love my sister. We have a very natural bond, and our personalities and characters are very compatible. We share many common experiences which have formed the way we both turned out, and we have been a witness to each other's lives. During those years in Harding and later in boarding school, there was no adult that could vouch for our lives, or speak on our behalves. We had to take care of ourselves. While it's true that she endured less humiliation and got more favour, especially from my father, in those times she was also exposed to dehumanisation and it must have affected the way she saw the world. There must be something weird about watching your sister being abused and being powerless to do anything real about it. We were left to our own devices and had to deal with many situations without parental or adult protection. And there are certainly horrible things that my sister went through, not because of her skin colour but because she was a girl growing up in a patriarchal society.

There are no absolutes in the world, this is what I have come to understand. In each of us exists the propensity to display heroic or cowardly behaviour, to stand up for what we believe in or to stand by and let it happen. No one knows what they will be or do when confronted with various situations. I did not know what I was capable of or the depth of my intolerance of injustice and unfairness until I witnessed my father set my mother up for some trouble. My parents married when my mother was too young. He was a strict man who ruled his home with a heavy hand.

My parents returned home one evening after work. My mother put the keys to the store on the dining room table and went to their room. When she returned from the room she went to the kitchen to check on the dinner we had cooked. While she was busy with that, I noticed that my father took the keys and hid them in his pocket. We all had dinner without incident and as we were concluding the dinner, my father asked my mother whether she had put the keys away. She responded in the affirmative. Then he asked her to fetch them. My mother went to the room and I could hear her rummage through the shelves of the dresser and the drawers of the wardrobes as she searched for those keys with escalating urgency and anxiety. I could feel something coming on.

My father called out to her a few times, and she responded from the room that she was still trying to locate the keys. She eventually came out of the room and relayed her surprise that the keys were not there. She then said that she might have left them on the table. We were still at the dining table at the time, and he asked her to show him where on the dining table she could have left them. My mother came to the dining table looking for the keys, and then we heard the thump of his hand against her cheek. He started to hit at her and taunted her about losing the keys. Inside of me was this torrent building up like a well being pressured from a volcanic eruption below. I could not explain where it came from and mainly did not know what to do about it. As my father continued to hit at my mother and taunt her, the well inside me rose with mounting pressure until I could not contain it any more. "Daddy took the keys, Mom, they are in his pocket." The pressure and the well inside me was stilled the moment those words left my mouth. I was at peace.

"Who was asking you? You think you too clever? Who asked you to come in between your mother and my affairs?"

I did not hear the rest of my father's words after that, they were just mutterings because he beat me all over my body and I woke the next day feeling very sore. I never regretted speaking up that day, neither did I regret the beating I got from my father that night. The pressure in me would otherwise not have been relieved if I had kept quiet. That protection and standing up for someone is perhaps the thing I most longed for from the people around me.

I still long for it today. I have the same feeling when I am not given the benefit of the doubt, even now. I have seen people make mistakes, big ones, but not suffer condemnation and emotional trauma from people around them, because they are human. The people in my life have done unthinkable things and said hurtful things to me; I try to step outside of my pain and let things go, and once again embrace them, because we all make mistakes. But it has been my experience that I am not allowed to make mistakes or have flaws, which is an impossibility of course, because I am flawed. But the retaliation and punishment that I receive in these times I feel do not fit the flaws or the perceived crime. Sometimes I could just be presumed to be flawed and then I am punished. Those punishments, particularly when they attack who I am naturally, my character and life decisions, are painful beyond measure. I have now reverted to writing when I feel this well of pressure building up inside of me.

Reflecting on this pressure build up from inside, some people direct it into themselves, whilst others direct it onto others. Those who turn on themselves perhaps self mutilate, they starve, they cry inside, and they drink. Others direct this pressure outside of themselves, they abuse others, display road rage that can lead to death of another, or beat others until that pressure inside them subsides.

The first time I deliberately and consciously directed this internal pressure to an action was after someone very close to me gave me a vivid and scathing description of who I was, and what I needed to be fixed. Every word dug into me like a flaming sword ignited on the mounts of Mordor. I felt a pressure build up inside of me and I walked around my house wondering what I needed to do to quell the torrent threatening to overwhelm me and end me. I was so tired of feeling so worthless, so wrong, so un-fixable, such a failure and so hated and misunderstood, and I swore to myself that I was not going to try one more thing to fix me. I was tired. I felt that I had reached the end of therapists, "fix me" books and the need to make people happy, or attempts to make me fit in, and I was not going to make another promise to ANYONE that I would try to be better. I needed to do something and I did not know what. I went into my kitchen, I started collecting pills and I drank them down. I went to my bed and I slept, feeling that I had no more need to do anything about anything and everything. I was at peace. I remembered Vena making jokes in that tall grass and I was smiling, and I felt warm inside, because Evy was embracing me.

The pills did not do their job, because I woke up three days later with a messy bed, an excruciating headache and a very damaged stomach. I had slept for more than seventy eight hours without waking up once. For at least a month after that, I could not put food into my mouth, because it was too painful and the blood in my stools frightened me no end. I would not go to a doctor, because I feared they would guide me into more therapy and hospitals. And I was having none of that!

But when I woke up and realised what my situation was, I guided myself both consciously and not to my laptop and I opened it and started to write. It was as if my being was saying, "If you don't feel heard, if you don't feel you have the benefit of the doubt, and if you feel unappreciated then write down what you feel and what you want to say. If you read back what you have written, then you have been heard." The first words I wrote were,

Sometimes
Someone just doesn't like you

In order to get along,
you have to constantly please and appease.
But no matter how much you do,
they will never like you,
never give you the benefit of the doubt.
They see the virtue in everyone else's side except
yours,
Never see you for who you truly are!
You have to make the calls, the apologies,
make the moves, turn a blind eye, ignore your place,
let them define the question, let them answer it,
control the mood, the pace, the rhythm...

You never at peace,
cause you are under constant scrutiny!
It's a Guantanamo of sorts!
Sometimes you can hear them waiting, watching
and anticipating your next flaw!
Tried, sentenced and found guilty in absentia,
with no need to produce evidence
Finally as you realise you can take the torture no
more,
that there ain't a darn thing you can do
to make them see you different...

Stop, let go, become the observer and watch things
unfold
It's a revelation what happens when you just stop
trying to appease, create and make things happen!

Achebe penned it well!

He did pen it well, and things did fall apart, the centre did not hold because I had stopped trying to hold the centre together. After this incident I was alone, many people left my life completely and others for a long time. And I promised myself on that day that I would not reach out to anyone. I would not apologise, beg, phone and ask anybody what was wrong or how they were doing. I would stop asking my close friends to come over, if they wanted to see me they could invite me to their place. And they could cook me dinners and invite me over to watch movies with them. I kept my phone on but I never made any calls or initiated any contact with anyone. I decided that I had been working too hard to make people happy and appease them, and I had had enough. I was running on empty and could not find a source to refuel me. I would not tell myself to "play bigger" and reach out to people who treated me like I was faeces. I had been doing this all along, and I was tired.

Some people never reached out to me after that and it took others months to get the message that I had changed, and I was done with that. It was their turn to realise any value in me and treat me like I was important to them, and if they could not do that I did not want them in my space, no matter how much I loved them. Any guilt twinges in me about my responsibilities to family or friends I quickly squashed with a loud shout to myself...STOP. And I stopped feeling any guilt.

I decided that I would rather be alone than have people around me who felt I were just wrong, and in whose presence I felt worthless. I was tired of apologising for who I was, no matter how awful everyone thought I was. I also decided that if no one appreciated who I was or what I had done for them, if they did not recognise the sacrifices I made for them to be what they could be, I would rather stop trying. At least if they said I did nothing for them or I was selfish, I would have earned the right to be called those names. I would gladly accept those labels, and I could show that the time I was spending was on those things that I love doing, on being me. I couldn't be accused of all of those things and still feel so trapped by responsibilities to others, and the constant worrying about whether I was doing or being anything to offend anyone. It is tiring and soul sapping. I also realised at that point that I needed to be religious about doing what I wanted to do, to make sure that I did not fall into my old habits of putting everybody else's needs ahead of mine.

The truth is that when you grow up being or feeling less than, you have to work so much harder at everything, just to get to par on the golf course of life. When you start at the first hole, you are already eighteen over par, and to make it, just to keep up, you have to sink birdies and eagles. To really win, even a par score on any one of the holes is just not good enough. You can try many courses, work very hard for very long, employ tremendous spells of concentration, practise hard for hours each day, endure hours in the blazing sun; and it is never good enough. And then one moment in your very tiring lifetime you realise that it requires too much effort, the decks are stacked too heavily against you. It is time to stop playing the game, or get busy changing the rules of the game.

It has been difficult for me throughout my life to be silent when I perceive an injustice to have taken place. It was time that I started defending myself first, and putting on the armour of the lawyer, to stand up for and defend my dignity, and my own right to be who I am. In this case silence and withdrawal was the first and most important step.

The incident with my mother and those "lost keys" would certainly not be the last time that I would stand up for my mother. I always felt the need to protect and care for her. Perhaps subconsciously I, or the *sabi* inside of me, believed that she deserved protection more than I did. I know that it was not because she gave me favour, because my younger sister was the recipient of that. I also realised that standing up for her would not bring me favour; it never did. Even after I got beatings from my father it was Evy who comforted me. Perhaps it was because it was the only way I could quell the torrent from inside me. Perhaps I was trying to show her or my father how to stand up for me and protect me. Perhaps because I felt that I had a place to retreat to in our backyard where I was fortunate to have found friends who actually loved me and liked being with me, and a place I felt I was okay. A place that balanced the brutality around me, and a place in which I was heard and really seen.

Sometimes I would watch my mother stare into an open space and her lips would move as she spoke to herself. I wondered if she had a secret place that she could retreat to where she was okay.

My father did many things to my mother which were difficult and painful for me to witness. One of his most brutal attacks was when he tied my mother to the back of one of his cars and drove at high speed with my mother's helpless body being dragged along tar road and on rugged terrain. My mother emerged from that incident with severe bruising all over her body and had to wear long sleeves and jerseys in hot weather to mask the brutality visible on her white skin for months. Another time my mother fell asleep in the car on one of our long road trips, and he stopped the car and beat and kicked my mother so hard that the sound from those blows filled the night sky with a distinctive eeriness. Every time I protested these actions against my mother I would be in for a brutal attack from my father. My Gogo once visited our home and cried when she saw the scarring from the beatings on my skin and that of my mother's. She rubbed ointment on my back and my legs and sang with tears in her eyes as she tried to comfort me. She was really the only woman who embraced me physically, besides Evy.

My mother often relates their brief courtship and the incidents of violence she endured at the time. He taught her how to drive, and during one of the driving lessons she stalled the car on a railway track. She could not get the car to start and there was a fast approaching train on the track to her left. My father punched her a few times and told her to do something fast or else they would both die. My mother describes the panic she felt with the oncoming train, the pressure of fists from my father in the car and the difficulty she had in getting the car to move forward. But eventually she did move the car, and says that she never stalled the car again after that incident. What a way to learn!

At that age I probably did not make the connection between what I was feeling and this overwhelming desire to be a lawyer. This is all I wanted to do when I grew up and finished with my schooling. Now I understand better the need to defend the defenceless, but perhaps I wanted to be a lawyer so I could in a legal and perceived intelligent way beat the oppressors and the bullies. It was impossible for me or my mother to match the power of a male beating you up or a grown woman torturing you at ten years of age. But I never doubted my intelligence and the ability to put a good argument together, even if it was in my own head and own world. I imagined in that world of mine that I was a powerful lawyer who could outwit anybody and in any court of law.

I joined the debating team at boarding school and found a way of expressing this need to be heard. I researched topics, put together what I thought were intelligent arguments and would readily participate in debates on various subjects from abortion and contraception to euthanasia. At this school we covered many topics, but never discussed the politics of the day. There is an invisibility about growing up the way I was – you never quite felt heard or really seen. But on that stage, when I would talk, people would listen. I remember one teacher commenting not only on the logic and creativity of the arguments I put forward, but also on my use of language and emphasis to make important points. That was probably the first compliment I received in my life, outside of Evy and Vena, and I revelled in my own thoughts about it. I have no trophies or certificates of excellence to attest to those accomplishments, and my name is not written on any school boards. But those compliments helped me to know what I wanted to do with my life. I wanted to be, needed to be, a lawyer.

When I got to my parents' home for the school holidays I would re-enact those debates for Vena and Evy, and Vena would always find ways to see the funny side of it. I would often also present a legal matter to them, and then present arguments before the jury. Being a lawyer was all I thought about for a long time.

There were some other activities I really enjoyed at boarding school. I inherited my father's rhythm and love of music and dance. I enrolled for piano lessons, joined the school choir, took ballet lessons, participated in school dramas, including Shakespeare productions, and took ballroom lessons. I also played tennis and badminton, tried hockey...but that sport was not for me. These activities brought much pleasure to me. In those days we had very limited options, a very different situation from what the children who were born after Nelson Mandela's release have. While it is true that there are so many glass ceilings for black people after Mandela's release, they do have more opportunities than we had. There are very few people of my generation and those before me who pursued careers and a life in music, drama, film, dance or tennis. If I could have made my own choices at the time, I would have been practising law, writing books, playing tennis and singing. Those are the things that felt most aligned to who I was and wanted to be. Before I came to this school, my time away from school was spent working and getting abused, but here I had the time to discover the wonderful world of music, dance, debate, drama and sport.

By my last two years in that school I had started to mellow out, just a bit; being occupied with these extra-mural activities, reading a lot and generally accepting what life around me was. I was a prefect in my final year of high school and really enjoyed the responsibility that came with it. Putting me in this position of responsibility in the school erased the excursions to the orchards and breaking into the kitchen at night. I used much of my time in the last school year to apply to the top universities in South Africa to study law, as well as to Oxford and Cambridge. Studying was not a major activity of mine, although my father would swear to all who would listen that his daughter was not clever, she just worked hard, at school at least! At home he thought I was lazy. Yes I did read a lot, but very little of it was for school. I am glad my father never got wind of that, because those books were my escape from a world which was not very kind to me, and provided many discussion topics for my long and animated visits to Evy. Books are important, because in each page lie adventures and discoveries about life and the world that grow your mind and give you options to explore areas that the people around you cannot participate in and taint.

I witnessed my siblings and many around me stressing after their last year of school about whether they would graduate. I never doubted it for one second, although I required a university entrance pass rate to enrol into the universities, which had all by that time written back to me and accepted my application, pending my final results. The end of that school year was a great time for me. I anticipated going to university in the following year and starting a new chapter in my life.

My parents had no knowledge or participation in the university application process. I had done that all on my own, and informed them that I would like to go to university to study law. I presented them with all the letters of acceptance and my father was pleased that I had taken the initiative. He always gave us children long lectures about furthering our education and how important it was in a country like ours to be educated, so that we could make something of our lives. About that my father was right. Education is an important step to transcending your personal and social circumstances, and my hope is that every child can have the opportunity to get a high-level education. But what I had witnessed growing up and later on in my own life is that it would not spare you from the humiliation and ugliness of discrimination. That requires a nationwide healing process for everyone, because we are all products of a racist, dehumanising and violent past.

The decision to go to university was not a choice, there was no alternative, it was just supposed to happen. My being knew that I needed education to survive and to make it on my own. The only area I knew, I just *sabi*'d that I could make it, was using my brain, and university was my gateway to freedom.

That was to be a wonderful vacation period for me. Although we returned home to the normal scene, shouting and hard work, there was something in the air and I could smell it. I did not mind anything happening at the time, as long as the road to university was not disrupted.

Better than

"When you are courting a nice girl an hour seems like a second. When you sit on a red-hot cinder a second seems like an hour. That's relativity."

Albert Einstein

Three years after enrolling at the University I graduated with my first degree. I was happy that I had a degree but I did not feel a great sense of achievement. In truth university academically was not a big challenge for me; I attended classes, did very little reading towards attaining that degree, but I sat the exams and I passed. My parents were proud that they had produced the first child on the paternal side of the family to graduate from university.

On the day of my graduation my parents attended the ceremony and must have been proud to be witnessing their offspring walking up those stairs to be capped by the dean of a premier university in South Africa, previously only attended by white people. They informed other family members from my father's side of my achievement and arranged for a dinner party at a restaurant, *Mike's Kitchen*, in Parktown, Johannesburg. After the graduation ceremony and the posing for pictures with my parents, we had a great time with family all wishing me the best for the future. The food was delicious and I was weirdly aware of the attention on me. That was the first celebration in my honour. I did not have birthday parties growing up and was not used to the attention on me. It was sixteen years since I started my first day at school at the age of four, and now soon to be twenty years old, by all accounts I was

109

an adult who would be responsible fully for myself, without having to account to anyone.

By the time I graduated with my first degree, my sister was married. I had grown accustomed to attending parties either in my sister's honour or because my father threw a bash for his family and friends. My sister had a sterling twenty first birthday party and the photographs attest to an elaborate affair in my home. My father also hosted a celebration of her engagement to her fiancé and the previous year, before my graduation, we had had a large wedding celebration for her. I felt strange having the focus and attention of family on me, but I was a very different person from the one who had enrolled in university three years before.

University was the place in which I discovered parts of myself and was exposed to many things that changed some of how I saw myself. My life got better when I was a student and I began to feel a sense of personal freedom. And although I was exposed to the brutalities of an oppressive regime more directly through student protest participation, there was a sense that I could do something to change things. I felt part of a bigger process that could make a difference to my life and those of the people around me. It was a great time for me and nothing before that could match its positive and progressive impact on my life. This was a time of great discovery and much laughter.

Bongi and I were registered for the same courses in the first and second year of our first degrees. She attended lectures as diligently as I did, and I took notes of all the key points the lecturers made. She often asked for my notes to do her daily review process, and my handwriting found itself improving as I knew that I would not be the only one to read them. After the first few weeks at university I realised that the key to passing courses was to listen to the lecturers and take notes that can be reviewed if necessary before the tests. I spent little time going into research or reading many of the suggested readings to enhance my understanding of the various subject matters. I very rarely reviewed the notes because I made a decision to listen attentively to the lecturers. Once I heard the concepts and understood them, I felt empowered to interpret them in tests. Because of this system, which worked for me, I had much time on my hands. This system did not produce a top student but it did produce a just-above-average scoring on tests, which in turn gave me a degree.

But Bongi had to work much harder than I had to, not because she could not grasp the concepts or because she was hard of hearing, but only because she struggled to hear the lecturers. These lecturers' accents were foreign to her and they spoke too fast, about advanced concepts, and there was no time to acclimatise to their accents. Bongi is one of the deepest and brightest thinkers I know. And it pained me to see how something that so many people take for granted could stand in the way of someone achieving their dreams. But that was not going to stand in Bongi's way, and she put in the hours, reading my notes, and the extra material to get to understand the material. Women in general, but black people in particular, truly have indelible spirits.

That was another feature of the South African landscape which enraged me to my core, and in university my anger and rage towards the people in my world that were unjust to me expanded to the country and later it was internationalised. Black people in general really did start most races against white people with a significant disadvantage. They were expected to compete with people who had significant advantages

111

over them, who received tutorship from people who looked and sounded the way they did, whose cultural realities were drawn on as a source of examples to bring theoretical concepts to life, and within institutions that were designed for them. My particular accident of history and experience that led me into a convent education with many white teachers, both local and foreign, and that endowed me with parental heritage which exposed me to different accents and races, I realised, made my academic experience different. But most people of colour did not have that exposure, and many who might have qualified to enter that university were not accepted because of a numbers game. At the time when Bongi and I attended this university, the quota system was still in place, so black people were a minority. The cultural and sporting associations on campus which are so important in developing and broadening one's world were mainly white with very little cultural diversity.

I joined other black students in starting the black student social organisation that would cater for black cultural, sporting and other activities on and off campus. At the time many of us had a strong view that those of us who made the quota should also participate and organise events within the community. We registered the organisation with the university and many black students joined. I was appointed secretary of the organisation and took my role seriously. I organised many social events with other office bearers, and there are two events which I took great pride in organising. The office bearers had met to discuss the types of events we would organise that year, and it was agreed that we should have two major functions each year, one cultural and the other social, whilst continuing to have the weekly sporting events in the communities around Johannesburg.

I began my second year at university as an eager seventeen year old. I was much younger than most of the people around me, and never spoke about my age to anybody, except for Bongi. Besides organising meetings for the office bearers, taking minutes and organising logistics for the local events, my first involvement with organising a big event was the trip to Lesotho. The student body agreed on a visit to Roma University, in the neighbouring country, Lesotho, as a means of forming closer ties with black students from other Southern African countries. We spent most of our time in the weeks leading up to the trip organising transport, assisting students who did not have passports and arranging with the student bodies in Lesotho for our accommodation. My brother, the one two years older than me, had by then moved to Johannesburg, where he was working after completing a trade course in boiler making. He visited one evening at the residence where I was staying. That evening we had dinner together with other female students and discussed the upcoming visit to Roma. By the end of the evening not only was my brother in love with one of the students, he had also found himself volunteering to drive one of the minibuses on our trip. Most of the students did not have a driver's licence so it was welcomed, because at the time the only other person with a licence was our treasurer. My brother is one of those people who lives his life on the edge, he creates something out of nothing, he makes things happen and does not take no for an answer. That evening he gave me too much money, but I accepted with a smile, because although I wanted for nothing because the university residence catered for all my basic needs, I did not have much cash. My father did not believe in spoiling his children.

The Roma experience was wonderful. It was the first time I had been out with a group of people to another country without my family and I could do whatever I wanted. I had my first drink on that trip and got tipsy. I laughed so much at everything and anything. We went to the local bars and hang out spots and had the time of our lives. I did not have any romantic interest at the time, but one of the office bearers who would be a lifelong friend of mine had been asking me out for months. I was not interested. At the time my interests revolved around politics, organising black social events and reading books not prescribed by the course work. I read so much when I was at university; most of the books were banned and for the first time many of us could access those books through the Black Student Movement members. I read and recited the speeches or writings of Kwame Ture, Steve Biko, Frantz Fanon, Martin Luther King, Nkwame Nkrume and Malcolm X, bought and read *Das Kapital* and other socialist and communist literature. I had a special affinity for Steve Biko because he also went to a boarding school in Natal like I did, then went on to university, and he could write. I have always been drawn to people who can write. But mostly it was because he was writing about what was relevant to me, inside of me, and he had written about what needed to be said. I also had an affinity for Kwame Ture, because he married a woman that I really liked – Miriam Makeba. I understood what he was saying in his speeches, but he was also born in the year of the snake, as I was. I have always had a thing for astrology.

This was my life and romance had no place for a long time. Because most of the books were banned, we would conceal them by covering them in brown paper and labelling them *Far From the Madding Crowd* or

Tess of the d'Urbervilles or other titles which were safe. I learnt the writings of the great icons of Black Resistance so well that I could recite pages of their text without referring to any paper.

One evening on the Roma trip, Stanley was playing guitar and all the students were singing the great freedom songs like *Senzeni Na? Somlandela, Makubenjalo and BIKO*. We sang *Nkosi Sikeleli Afrika* a lot because it was banned at that time, and today it is the national anthem of this country. I performed two great speeches with Stanley playing the guitar in the background: "*I have a dream*" from Martin Luther King and selected extracts from Steve Biko's "*I write what I like*" works. We felt united by our heritage and felt a great reverence for these icons who had gone before us.

We also partied hard on that trip, visiting bars, taking them over because of our numbers, and dancing to the beats of Sipho Hotstix Mabuse, Brenda Fassie and Miriam Makeba. We had no place for sleep on that trip, we were all discovering each other, what we had in common, and we felt free. We returned from Lesotho feeling good about our trip. Later we got into trouble with the university authorities because we had taken an additional university-owned minibus without asking for permission. But none of us minded that because we had memories that no one could take away. The success of the trip and the talks on campus about it saw an increase in the membership of the organisation, so by the time we organised the on-campus social event the atmosphere was abuzz with possibilities.

In the last term of the year we hosted an evening function where we hired a disk jockey and invited the legendary singer Brenda Fassie to perform. It was a magical evening. The students arrived in their numbers with partners all dressed up in glittering evening wear. I

115

wore the white dress that my sister had worn for her twenty first birthday celebrations. It was a stunning dress, strapless with white and silver tassels adorning it from top to bottom, and those delicate tassels created their own movement and dance patterns whenever I moved. I was feeling on top of the world.

I had invited my eldest brother's girlfriend, who had given birth to a beautiful baby girl, and her younger brother to the function. Her brother and I had been attracted to each other from the first time we met, a few months earlier. He was a handsome young man with a magic smile and a set of eyebrows that made me take notice of him. He had voluptuous lips and a few times I stared at them intently and wondered how it would feel being kissed by those lips. I danced with him and a few guys from our organisation through the night. I drank a few Esprits that night and the tipsiness enhanced my enjoyment of that evening. I can say that was the best evening of my life up to then. The evening ended with David and I sharing a sensual kiss that stirred things inside of me that I had never felt before. It felt forbidding, exhilarating and breathtaking all at the same time. I was bidding them farewell when David whispered in my ear, "You are beautiful". I froze up instantaneously and walked away from the car back to the residence and when I reached my room I began to cry.

Why did he have to spoil a perfectly good evening? In eighteen years of my life I had never heard those words associated with me, except for one evening after a political reading session when Thabo said, "You have a smile that keeps me up at night…You are beautiful". Thabo was a fellow student who took Sociology classes with me and had befriended me. We often spoke after lectures but when he said those words, I gave him a look that would sink a ship, walked away from him and never thought about it again, until that night. Although I saw Thabo almost every day during classes and at the student canteen, he sensed that he should never say those words to me again.

There was a kind of freedom that I felt with not being associated with a male, or being in love. I had friends who would spend hours stressing and crying about some boyfriend doing or not doing what they would expect. I saw girls endure gruesome regimens of diets and near-death exercise routines. I witnessed even more girls being mean to each other because they thought someone was after their man. I saw a girl bleeding profusely from a backstreet abortion because she had gotten pregnant by a famous singer who was married. I was discovering life and just couldn't imagine myself being subjected to that stuff. It just was not for me. At the back of my mind I wanted a degree, and that was my first priority. I wish I could say that I worked day and night to obtain that degree but I did not. I had figured out a minimum input system that would ensure I would graduate, and allowed me much time to be involved in other pursuits. But I never factored boys, kissing and sex into that extra time. After the night of my first real kiss, I stayed away from the house of my brother's girlfriend. It would only be after university that I would see David again.

There are people you meet in your life that will make an indelible mark on your life and who bring out the you inside of you. They hold up a real mirror for you to see who you are, and although it is an uncomfortable process, an image emerges in that mirror for you to see through less tainted eyes and for you to embrace and integrate into the you that you became in order to

117

survive. For no matter how strong you are, and no matter how many worlds you escape into from a harsh world, or how good you know you are at intellectual pursuits, the view of yourself is dominated by what you see reflected in the eyes, words and actions of the people around you.

But to some people you are not invisible. They see you in some instances even better than you are able to see yourself. They provide a safe place for your coming out process and you just know that they will always be there. These are phenomenal people and I had the good fortune of getting to know a phenomenal woman when I attended this university; this is Bongi.

Bongi was formed from the depths of the source of wisdom itself, and her life of truth, love, understanding and patience is testimony to these origins. She is a rare gem, because only gems so precious are formed from such depths. The first time I met her she saw me and it is rare that I meet people who really see me. Who see beneath the smile, the frown, the fear, the confidence, the jokes or the word. There was a deeply comforting and yet frightening feeling in knowing that she saw me. We have been friends for more than half my life now and our love and friendship will never die. This I *sabi*. It is one of the things that I know without a doubt will never change, because our souls are linked and tied to each other and nothing on this planet could change that. She was the first person that I had certainty about. This connection does not need daily visits, lots of phone calls, validations or arguments to sustain itself. It is a deep bond and an eternal love and it can never die because it is self sustaining. It thrives and grows on the basis of the two souls' existence.

My friend held up a mirror to me with love and patience. The process was not easy for me and I struggled to grasp the view that I was perhaps different

118

from what I thought I was. It is a painful birthing process complete with tearing and labour pains. Sometimes it is even easier to accept that you are what other people have said you are, rather than embrace a new reality, because that is the world you know and a world in which you have learnt to survive. But at the end of the day, it has been a survival, and in order to start living you have to look in the mirror and see the real you. Sometimes the conditioning has been so embedded that in some areas even when you look in the mirror you can only see what was reflected from your family or your torturer's eyes. *Sabi* is very powerful, especially if the *sabi* happens when you are very young. In some instances, it is very difficult, if not impossible to un-*sabi*.

The first view reflected in that mirror was my skin. My skin was a very powerful and all embracing identifier. I was first black before I was a woman or any other thing you could discover if you ever got beneath the skin. The skin had masked who I was even from myself and it masked who I was from everyone else around me, except from Bongi. She saw me. I remember when she first commented on my flawless skin. I was confused when she mentioned flawless to describe my skin. She referred to a characteristic of my skin that had nothing to do with colour. She was pointing to the texture and feel of it, and until that point I had never thought of a skin beyond its colour. Sure I did biology and studied the skin and knew all the physiological characteristics of it but I never related any of those to mine.

My skin was who I was and there were words and phrases used to describe it like dark, black or really dark. I looked in the mirror when I returned to the residence that evening and decided to strip myself of all my clothes and look at my skin. Now, truth be told, I had avoided mirrors all my life and that day looking into the mirror was like drilling a tooth without anaesthetic. I fought through the screeching sound and excruciating pain of the drilling and studied my skin. Slowly I began to see my skin beyond its colour and I realised that there were no scars, no blemishes and no acne at all…it was indeed flawless, except for the scars from the beatings. I thought back to my sister's skin and remembered that she had some marks on her face and considered my younger sister's face and saw pimples. I had none of this. I went to my notes from the previous lecture, found a blank piece of paper and wrote down "I have flawless skin". I had found something beautiful about my skin.

A few days later my friend Bongi and I were having dinner together at the residence, Jubilee Hall, and I was relating to her my discovery. She laughed at my comic interpretations of my discovering these new qualities in front of that mirror. She has a wide mouth and when she laughs, her whole face lights up. I laughed with her that day and felt drawn to her spirit. When we were walking to the dessert table to get some treats, she looked at me squarely in my eyes and said "You are a very special person". My person could not digest those words. My ears heard them but that is as far as they got and bounced back into the air before they could pass my middle ear. I made a joke about the dessert, decided to take two different types and ate them up. I told her I had lots of homework and went back to my room. I am sure she knew that I was not truthful about my reason for leaving the dining hall, because she knew my self-developed academic system and it never involved doing homework. I stayed in that room all evening and eventually fell asleep.

Life continued as usual on campus for a few weeks after that exchange in the dining hall. I figured out a way in which I could give Bongi my course notes from the lectures I had attended, share a table during lunch that involved other people, and left no room for discussion about mirrors, flawlessness or being special. This went on for weeks and my friend Bongi allowed me to display my denial, probably hoping I would come around and return to a table over dinner with just the two of us there, or invite her to my room for long evenings of chatter. But it never happened and my friend decided that if she did not make the move to break this superficial connection and eerie *impasse*, I would have probably left the university in that state. And if indeed that is what she was thinking, she would have been right. I did not identify with those words she had uttered, so how could I even find a way of discovering what they could mean, and least of all look in the mirror to find "special"?

One morning she knocked on my door, and this time I opened the door. I could sense it was her. She smiled and said she needed help with some of my notes. As I was explaining the notes, she *sabi* and I *sabi* that she had no need to hear my explanations. But we continued for about half an hour discussing those negligible notes. When we were done she said she was hungry and that I should join her for breakfast. We ate together that day and discussed everything and nothing. We did not venture into any talks about me, she had sensed how fragile I really was and how I had gone into a state of silence and routine to contain and mask those things that I could not even understand. But that morning was to break the weeks of superficiality that had defined our communication. I have learnt since then that this is my pattern, when I encounter something that is unfathomable to my being, I become civil, distant and impenetrable. I retreat into my world, I go away.

Bongi took the lead in the next series of exchanges that would be both epic and profound for me. The aftermath of those exchanges would lead to awakenings deep inside of me and would spur on life changing events for me. She told me aspects of her life that I had never imagined before. She was a child of the June 1976 uprisings in Soweto. She had left the country for Swaziland, a neighbouring country that had received many of the youth that fled after those infamous uprisings that claimed the lives of so many youths of South Africa. She told me of her treacherous journey to Swaziland with promises from the youth leaders that they would receive training and join *Umkhonto we Sizwe*, the armed struggle wing of the African National Congress. She explained how she and the youths who had fled were filled with a burning desire to fight for the liberation of the country and how that was the only option that was open to youth at the time. She told me of the anger that raged inside of her for the unjust system and of the equal passion she had inside of her to bring the apartheid government to its knees. I could identify with each syllable in every single word that left her mouth that day. I had been ten years old at the time, living under the Cruella regime when Bongi had experienced these things. Also the time when I began to build a rage at cruelty, torture and injustice and the overwhelming feeling of being powerless against those who ruled my life. She had an outlet, I did not. And it was evident that that rage was contained inside me and had not found expression but hers had been given a path, from which she emerged calm, knowing and at peace with herself and the world.

I considered her life and marvelled at it. I pondered the immense passion and conviction she had to take this journey, albeit driven by intolerable cruelty and unfairness, but what impacted on me most was her strength of character to make a choice for herself to return to South Africa after being holed up in Swaziland for some time. I admired this woman before my very eyes and wished I could be more like her. I could see that her life experiences had refined her, but I could also see that some innocence and a confidence had been taken away from her. She and I both share a confidence about our thinking ability, but a nervousness about linking those ideas, which were profound, to ourselves publicly.

And now here she was getting a degree at a premier university, having to work harder than most people because she could not decipher accents of a people who were responsible for the death of many of her neighbours and friends. Some realisations in life wake you up to a different way but also increase your rage at a system that created all of this in the first place.

I was very angry at the indefensible system into which we were both born. A system in which, although she could notice a flawless skin, still subjected us both to a painful existence because our skin colour was deemed inferior. I was angry. I joined both the leftist and populist campus organisations at the time, as well as any others that were opposed to injustice. I learnt more of the Palestinians' struggle, which mirrored ours, and joined in marches against the Israeli led occupations and the murderous machinery of the Israeli military regime. I was choked by teargas and endured beatings from police as they moved to squash student riots. We had very charismatic student leaders on campus and their calls to march into Jorissen Street to show our disdain for the apartheid government and the detention of comrades without trial, and the deaths of many activists in police custody, moved many students, like myself into the streets.

There is a sweeping power to a mob, wherein you are a cog or a part of a whole. When you are in a mob situation, marching with others with whom you share a strong conviction for something bigger than the self, individual thought leaves and is replaced by a collective thought process. No one person could run straight into a well equipped and armed police force as brutal as the apartheid police on her own, but when you are with others, your thinking and decision making process gives way to something bigger than yourself. The charismatic and passionate leaders would be followed without question, because in that moment they are the conductor of this orchestra of collective thought, in which the individual has no place.

This collective consciousness through the mob has also led us down some very ugly roads. There is an experience in this time that presented me with a vivid and innate sense of what I could or could not do. I was part of a student political gathering on the university lawns, when one of our leaders announced that a student had been identified as a spy working for the Special Branch, an *impimpi*. The alleged spy was paraded on the steps of the lawns and people were angry and disgusted that one of our own people could betray the cause. I joined in with the slogans, loudly and fervently condemning the spy until my full voice gave way to rasps. The anger and disgust of the students at the gathering reached fever pitch and the collective conscious, led by the main speaker, steered us to a decision to necklace the spy. A tyre appeared in the middle of the gathering and the mob beckoned the speaker to bring him to face his fate. From that moment on my individual consciousness disassociated itself form the collective conscious and I became an observer for a few minutes. From the outside looking in I saw the power of collective action and my being screamed

STOP! I started screaming "Stop!" and pushing my way towards the spot where the speaker was, in an attempt to urge him to stop. I was possessed by the need to stop this action, and I noticed that others were doing the same and making strides in attempting to stop the necklacing. In the end, the killing of the alleged spy did not take place. But that moment changed me.

Repulsive and violent systems and regimes like apartheid breed revolting and violent responses, even if the responses to alter the status quo are birthed in noble intentions. The history of necklacing in South Africa is a blotch to our history and something we must face and accept as a horrid waywardness on the road to freedom that we could have done without. I have debated this subject with many friends and acquaintances over the years and no one disagrees that those were some of our ugliest moments as a nation.

Mob justice no matter where and how it is meted out, is a step back for mankind. The very thing you fight is the very thing you become, unless you desist from walking down that road. Mob justice is not peculiar to South Africa, but a phenomenon experienced around the world. A man is lynched for allegedly desecrating the Holy Quran in the village in Dadu district of Sindh by a mob of some two hundred people in front of the local police station. Four students from the University of Port Harcourt left campus for the village of Aluu. Within minutes of their arrival a rumour spreads that the students were there to steal and a mob stripped them naked, beat them with sticks and rocks, wrapped car tyres around their necks and burnt them to death. This killing was filmed and posted on the web. Scholars estimate that in Europe, about fifty thousand people, eighty per cent women, were burnt alive after falling victim to the infamous witch hunts. Over five thousand horrific lynchings took place in the

United States, one of which inspired the poem by Abel Meeropol, which became the lyrics of the song *Strange Fruit* performed by Billie Holiday. I always get a strange sense come over me when I listen to that song. Strange fruit indeed!

Those necklacings, when they took place, made us no better than those who hung and burnt our people who were taken from our shores as slaves.

I have since spent much time considering the options of the oppressed and disenfranchised. Does it really come down to just two options – fight or surrender as Nelson Mandela stated in his treason trial speech in 1964, when explaining the decision of the African National Congress to take up arms?

"We had no doubt that we had to continue the fight. Anything else would have been <u>abject surrender</u>. The time comes in the life of any nation when there remain only two choices – submit or fight. We shall not submit and we have no choice but to hit back by all means in our power in defence of our people, our future, and our freedom."

This is the choice that the people before us made when they began the armed struggle, or when they decided to defy and resist. I wonder what the significant deciding factor is that makes people choose fight, no matter what form it takes, armed or peaceful, instead of surrender. Perhaps it is a sense that you are worth more than the circumstances around you reflect, or more than the prevailing voices and images that reflect who you are, to you. The motivation for that sense must come from within, from a part of you that is untainted and immune to that which says you are what you are not. Surrender is a pact you make with the oppressor that they are superior, and you are inferior. That they deserve a place in the sun, and that you don't.

But herein lies the irony, when you access this place of untainted truth. Mortality must become a strange bedfellow that you accept and welcome like the comfort of a friend's embrace. And perhaps the willingness to lie with this strange bedfellow and accept it requires an unshakable or resolute belief in something, a cause or an ideal much bigger and more eminent than you are as an individual. In the end you have to surrender the individual to the magnanimous, and disregard the individual wants, whims and idiosyncrasies. This must be the point at which freedom is almost palatable.

So the statements following those fight or surrender statements in the Nelson Mandela treason trial speech are perhaps not out of place.

"I have cherished the ideal of a democratic and free society in which all persons live together in harmony and with equal opportunities. It is an ideal which I hope to live for and to achieve. But if needs be, it is an ideal for which I am prepared to die."

Death found many people who were prepared to die for a better world, and some, like Nelson Mandela, got to see the other side, albeit with tremendous sacrifice. All but ten thousand days of sacrifice. But the real freedom he experienced may have been before South Africa experienced its own; it was when he reached the point of accepting that he would surrender to death to fight for a cause. I have in later years replaced my sadness with an admiration for those great people who have fallen in pursuit of a better life for others that followed them, an admiration firstly for their courage and selflessness, and secondly for the peace and freedom they must have felt when they made their choice. Great people like Steve Biko, Robert Sobukwe, Thomas Sankara, Martin Luther King and Huey P Newton must have died a peaceful death. They all welcomed that strange bedfellow long before they met their actual death.

I further ponder whether people who walk into danger and not fear death feel that they have nothing to lose, or is it that they have something to gain? I have battled with these concepts for a while and spend considerable time thinking them through.

My time at the university was filled with lots of readings, debates, discussions and thinking about life and the world. Sometimes these were through organised formations in the movements I had joined and sometimes there were informal reading and discussion groups, notably those discussing Marxist writings. I mostly enjoyed the one-on-one discussions when we could relate these ideas to everyday life, and had little patience for people who walked around with ideologies under their arms, and it is all they spoke about, whether at parties, on the sport fields or on the street while waiting for a bus.

When I joined other student activists undertaking door-to-door campaigns, linked to the United Democratic Front, to the townships to broaden the movement, or to get people involved in boycotting certain things, I was always interested in being able to tell people how it would affect them on a personal level, on a family level, on a community level and on a country level. I was never able to sell ideas very well unless I understood how it could affect people on these levels.

I belonged in that space at that time and there was no place that I would have rather been. It was a tremendous time of growth for me.

After I graduated, I was not entirely sure what to do next. I felt that the three years there had been a time of significant enlightenment and growth, but most of that came from everything that was happening around me rather than what I learnt at university during course work. Later I got to understand that the education I received through the Bachelor's degree did provide a framework through which I viewed the world, and did influence my understanding of the world and its political, social and economic systems.

The reality is that I felt I was doing the best with what I was presented. When I went to the university to enrol, my parents came with me. I went to the law faculty tables to get the forms needed to complete the registration process. And as if my father had not paid attention, listened or participated in any of the talks that I had in that house about my intentions to study law, and my animated demonstrations on how I would practise law, he announced right there and then that no daughter of his was going to do law. He went on at length about how lawyers are liars and that he could not sponsor anyone to become a liar. I was shattered by those utterances, but knew right away when he was serious. I bit my lip and quickly thought of plan B. It was customary when applying at the university to give three options for studies. My first was law, second was a Bachelor of Arts and the third I cannot recall. So without flinching I went to the arts faculty section and they explained that I had to select courses.

I had no idea what anthropology was, so I chose it first. I also opted for political studies, sociology and psychology. There was no structure or logic to the choices I made. This was not why I wanted to come to university and whatever there was to study, I would have, regardless of the topic. So when I graduated, I did not have any major feelings of accomplishment.

129

During my time at the university I visited the main court in Johannesburg and would listen to many of the cases being presented there. I would live vicariously through those attorneys and I learnt much from the hours spent listening to courtroom proceedings. I had front row seats on two occasions when Winnie Mandela appeared in court for some anti-apartheid activities. I also imagined that I would have done a much better job on some of the cases. Of course I realised that I was a back seat lawyer, but at the time I was sure how I would have done things differently.

I got on very well with some of the student leaders at university, two of whom were studying law. I was a little envious and really wished I could have been doing what they were doing. One of them is counsel for the arrested and injured mine workers of the Marikana massacre, where police shot and killed some forty striking miners in post apartheid South Africa. It has since emerged that many of the deceased were shot in the back. Police brutality has been with us for a long time. I watched police brutalise my father growing up, I watched them beat my brothers, I was a victim of police beatings at university and witnessed many other students getting beaten up. Many people experience this reality every day. The sad case of the Mozambican driver who was tied behind a police van and dragged through the streets and later beaten up by police, causing his death, is not new to South Africa. The ENCA, the African news station, interviewed a security consultant who had worked in the police force before and after independence, and he said that that kind of treatment of civilians was not new, it happened before and after apartheid. The only difference is that people now have access to phones that are able to record the atrocities committed by police.

Perhaps in the same way that access to money does not change people, but only exemplifies and expands who they really are, that which we are in our homes is exemplified and magnified when we are given positions of power over other people's lives.

But my passion, obsession, intrigue and love affair with law has never diminished. My favourite television series are legal ones –*Perry Mason*, *Law and Order*, *Ally McBeal*, *Franklin and Bash*, *Matlock*, *LA Law* and the *Good Wife*; I have watched every episode of the television series *Suits* and sincerely wish to be more like Harvey. Perhaps the legal series that rates in the top three of my all time favourites is *The Practice*. I saw myself reflected in each of those characters and was taken by the breadth and depth of the issues they explored through Bobby, Ellenor, Eugene, Jimmy, Rebecca and Lindsay's characters, exposing the duality and imperfections of both the human condition and the legal system. This is the practice that I probably would have worked for if television was real life. And who cannot love Kathy Bates in *Harry's Law*?

But in the mid nineteen eighties other people had much power and control over one's life, and you had to make the best of what you were presented with. And here at this place there were reminders of how fortunate I was to be studying at all. My father's self built riches, my academic ability and my resourcefulness in applying to every university I suppose put me in this place. The more I learnt how the world worked, and the more I was exposed to the impact apartheid had on the lives of black people, the more I saw how fortunate I was to be at a university like this, and I began to see that the trajectory of my life would be different from that of many of the people I had met along the way. I also got to see how that boarding school, although harsh in many aspects, and being away from home since the age of four had prepared me for the independence and self motivation that university required.

The exposure to different races through my mother's family, our family church, my father's business and personal connections, and teachers in that boarding school meant that I was familiar with various races and accents so I did not struggle the way that others did who had a different upbringing from mine. Even though I could see the negative effects of not having adult guidance and protection from an early age, and being away from my parents, I also noticed at university how much I did on my own. At university you were left to your own devices, and you had to set the pace for your academic schedule. I realised that I had been responsible for myself and my life for a long time, and even though the environments were oppressive and people had control over me, I had implemented various systems to cope and survive since a very tender age.

I also got to appreciate and understand the concept of *better than*. At the boarding school there was nothing about the food that was good and sometimes, most times, you could see the worms in the porridge we had to eat. It was a far cry from what my home offered. But I realised that it was better than Harding, where my sister and I were responsible for cooking and had to endure forced feeding spells. Yes, we had duties but those could not compare to the Harding experience. So it was better than. It was also better that the attention was not focused on me as much; there were too many girls for me to be singled out as much as in Harding.

Also, during the boarding school years the beatings were reserved for holiday periods. So there was a welcomed three-month-at-a-time hiatus from beatings. This certainly was better than. Whilst the boys in the school were subjected to beatings, the girls did not suffer that fate as much; we only had to work, and even then it could not compare to the tempo of Harding or home. My own love of cultural and sporting activities was only revealed in boarding school because prior to that period my life revolved around that house where we stayed, and the familiar pattern of beatings, insults, humiliations, cooking, visits to Dr Fixit, cleaning and visits from the male in that house at nights.

University was way better than. The only punishment was failure academically, which meant repeating a year or being excluded from university. I belonged here, because this place rewarded independence and passing. I was beginning to see that each place I moved to was better than. During the varsity years, the beatings at home subsided significantly, but were to be replaced by other actions from my father which I sometimes battled with.

My father did not go to university, so he did not really grasp the independence that I was afforded, but on occasion he would cotton on. He no longer had the report card system from high school that commented on my behaviour, instead it was merely percentages or grades next to each subject. There was no other way of measuring or commenting on behaviour, only academic excellence. I also was the only family member at the university, so no one could report back about my activities. My father felt less in control of me, so he initiated new forms of investigations to attempt to know what was happening in my life.

The first one he attempted was calling me at various times in the evening at the university residence. If he called and could not reach me, he thought I was out doing something wayward. When he did reach me, he would spend much time on the phone shouting at me and imagining all sorts of things, accompanied by insults. Those one way phone calls were filled with name calling that did not surprise me. After the phone calls I would go on with my business as usual. Well, not quite; in reality I found it difficult to reconcile my own growth and the personal freedom I began to feel with the treatment from my father. This led me down various dangerous paths.

But the holidays were tough in those years, he would go over all incidences again and I would sit there and listen to my father relate his imaginings about what I was doing. Mostly they had to do with sexual behaviour. He said he could not understand how I was passing, with the lifestyle I was living. Of course he was referring to the lifestyle that he had made up in his imagination. Perhaps he would have been more vocal, if that was possible, if he knew what I was really up to. In his mind, the only way I could have been passing is if I was sleeping with my lecturers. He would go on at length about how I was an embarrassment to his mother's name. I wish I could say that those comments and insults did not get to me, and that my own found freedom and growth at the university balanced those comments. The reality is that they hurt me no end.

I knew there was a disjuncture between my life there, my history, what was inside of me, and what was reflected in the eyes of the people I encountered in the different spheres of my life. I was studying psychology and because it was a major course, I began to see the impact of childhood trauma and abuse in the examples we were given. I understood the concepts and could pass tests, though I never could relate these to my own life. I learnt about multiple personalities, schizophrenia and other mental diseases. I did not realise it at the time, but I had boxed my own feelings and my experiences into silos which were not accessible to the people around me, and especially not to myself. It was as if my life had many floors or layers and the university experience was one floor that was almost independent of the other layers. When I went home, I left the me of this university floor and entered another floor where a different me operated, to a different landscape and different rules. I did not speak much about university at home, because it was a foreign concept there and because "you think you too clever" was too often used to silence me. I also began to realise that there are arguments I could have in my head, or my other world, that needed to stay there and not be brought onto this floor. Because I had read a lot in my life I had a relatively wide general knowledge of various topics. My father also had bought the entire volumes of the *Britannica Encyclopaedia* and I loved those books. We would also receive the annual updates, which were put on our bookshelf. I would read through them whenever I had free time. So when there was a question raised at home about some general knowledge issue, even if I knew the answer, I would not offer it. I would rather volunteer to find the answer in the encyclopaedia, and would read it out and sound surprised by what I was reading. I had a distinct sense that people around me did not really think that I deserved to have the capacity of intellect, and I have always played down my achievements in their presence. Recently I told a family member that I had created a body of work that changed the way a national priority was perceived and the country's response to it, and that this work had led to the development of a strategy put before parliament. I also told her that a senior manager in government attributed a great part of how she advanced to great heights to the role I played in her life. She cried and that made me cry too, and I did not know why either of us were crying.

My first visit to a therapist was at university. The campus had a facility that provided both medical and mental health facilities to students. One day I saw a brochure on the steps of the main campus building and kept it in my room for some time before I had the will to visit. I went to see the therapist a few times but it did not really work for me, so I stopped the visits. On reflection, I suppose I had not allowed myself or anyone else to penetrate the different silos, layers or floors that constituted my life. And presumably the therapist did not have the skills to help me to penetrate them or identify that they existed at all. I remember wanting to laugh at some of the sessions, and tried really hard not to laugh out loud. It was all very funny to me and I realised that I could not be a therapist.

I kept passing tests, and this put my father's theories about me in a tailspin. In his mind university study was difficult and required absolute dedication and there was no way in which I could be passing if his imaginings were spot on about my lifestyle. He did not know how to handle this period. When he found evidence that could corroborate his views of my lifestyle, all hell broke loose. My siblings still begrudgingly refer to the Cape Town trip that turned out atrociously for all. Holiday travel, particularly in December, was something my father loved to do. He had various minibus type of vehicles that could accommodate his children. On this particular trip I showed my brother a few photographs from the Lesotho trip and we were relating some of the events to our other siblings. My father stopped the car and asked to see the photographs. The details of what he did and said are perhaps not as important as the impact. We spent more than twenty hours on the road before we reached Cape Town.

In all of that time my father was the only person who really spoke. He went on and on about the kind of child I was, and his monologues would be interrupted by a question.

Who gave you permission to go on this trip?

No one, Dad.

Then he would talk for twenty minutes

Silence for about five minutes

We all hope that the silence means it is over

Do you think you are at university to play?

Silence

I am talking to you! Do you want me to stop this car and take off my belt?

No, Dad.

No what?

No, I am not at university to play, Dad.

Then he would talk for twenty minutes

Silence for about five minutes

We all hope that the silence means it is over

Are you pregnant?

No, Dad.

Are you busy with boys?

No, Dad.

So you don't see boys?

No, Dad.

Ha...ha...ho...ho...So you mean there are no boys there?

There are boys, Dad, but I am not busy with them.

Then he would talk for twenty minutes

Silence for about five minutes

We all hope that the silence means it is over

Then he turns to my mother

Mary, did you know about this?

No, I did not know about the trip, I have just found out

Ha...ha...ho...ho...

Then he talks for too much time, explaining how nice it would be to have a wife who does not keep things from him. Does she realise that she is digging a grave for me? Does she ever take the time to talk to me and check to see if I am not sleeping with boys. Did she even notice if there were stripes behind my knees? It was believed that women develop stretch marks behind their knees, above the calf muscle, if they are no longer virgins! He was sure she did not even notice, because she is too busy covering up things and spoiling these children...All of them! She needed to be careful of me, because I was too clever for my own liking.

Silence

Do you think you can fool us with that psychology?

No, Dad.

I should never have agreed to that psychology. I am suffering because of it.

Silence

So you too clever to reply.

No, Dad.

I can't believe I let this child do psychology!

Silence

What are you saying?

Nothing, Dad.

Oh, you cannot reply, because I am stupid and you are clever?

No, Dad.

What did you want to do with this psychology?

Make us a fool?

No, Dad.

So tell me why?

I didn't want to do psychology, Dad, I wanted to do law.

Oh, so you prefer being a LIAR?

No, Dad.

Are you saying I chose this psychology?

No, Dad.

Did I choose that psychology? So what are you saying? You see, Mary, I have been telling you that this child is confusing us with that psychology of hers. She thinks she is too clever! But you don't listen to me, she will show you with that cleverness of hers!

Silence

Now you can't answer me?

What was the question, Dad?

Then he stopped the car in a stage of rage.

Do you want me to get out of this car so you can take over because you are the clever one? We should all be listening to you?

No, Dad.

The reality is that I knew I should not have asked my dad to repeat the question. But I could not help myself. A simple "No, Dad", even though I genuinely did not know what the question was, would have sufficed. And even if he had said "No what?" I could have said, "No, I am not too clever, Dad." But I said it. Perhaps it was because at that stage I really did see the funny side of it. I imagined this scene in a comedy or on stage. I had been watching quite a few comedies and drama productions, both at the university and at the Market Theatre and I could genuinely see Eddie Murphy, who I had recently discovered through a movie where he swore a lot, performing a role. I learnt the use of profanities through the first movie of his I watched and began using these profanities quite often to express disgust or anger. Many times previously, whether it was through the beatings or when I just escaped into my own world, I would create elaborate scenes, many of them were very funny to me and Vena when we acted them out.

When we reached Aliwal North in the Eastern Cape, my dad got out of the car to use the restroom and my siblings gave me a tongue lashing. Can't I think of anything that would make my father stop? Why did I have to go to Lesotho, now they must all suffer for it? Why did I have to show those photographs, when I know how my father was? That was not a very clever move now, was it? Just say sorry and that you will never do it again. Do something, just anything, but make it stop! I could feel their frustration, although I had been creating comedic scenes in my world, they were not enjoying this monologue with smatterings of "No, Dad."

My family as a whole loved music and all the cars were equipped with facilities to play music on cassettes that my father bought or that we had recorded at school, or that my older siblings had recorded for us. Our trips, whether to Maputo, Durban, Cape Town or on the way to church some eighty kilometres away, always involved music, until this one. I devised a plan and before my father got back into the car I loaded the Louis Armstrong cassette he loved so much into the audio deck. When he got back into the car and turned the ignition the sounds of Satchmo filled the car. My plan was working, because my dad started moving his head according to the music ever so slightly. Even his lips were moving just a bit to the lyrics *Well hello Dolly...You looking fine Dolly*. I looked around to my siblings and made excited gestures indicating that things were better. But few of them believed it, although they hoped it so. That state of anticipation, waiting to see if my father was done with the monologue and question time, lasted through the first song. I think it was the slightly long pause before the next song started, that caused all the trouble. At that point my father said, "Mary, put that thing softer."

I was thinking in the toilet, Mary, that this child really thinks that we are her fools. We are working for her to get educated, and she is making us fools. My own money is making me a fool! I am sure we are laughing stocks all over the place. Everyone must know what she is up to in that place, it's only us...the fools.

Silence, with very soft Satchmo playing in the background, barely audible, he would start up again.

Where did we go wrong, Mary? Where? Maybe I should have let her go to Oxford? Maybe we should have let her do law? Ho ho! But can you imagine she would be worse than this. Worse, Mary, I am telling you! Can you imagine how she would be confusing us. And telling lies? Is it this thing about being black that is getting to her? When she came crying to me about how those people treat her at the boarding school, I told her that I had to deal with white people whose hair flowed like silk in that school I went to. I told her to be strong. She must be strong! What else can she do?

While he was speaking, I thought that playing *Manneburg*, the track put out by pianist and jazz musician Dollar Brand, later known as Abdullah Ibrahim, would have been a much better option. Not only did my father love Ibrahim, who was born on the same day, month and year as he was, but that track took up an entire side of a cassette and it would have calmed my father down.

This scene continued until we reached Cape Town, the birthplace of Ibrahim. By that time my father had been talking for a long time, and he had run out of things to say, or was tired of repeating the same questions to me over and over again. I still have those photographs today, and each time I laugh when I see them. There are some memories that never fade, and this is one of those, for all of the people who were on that road trip.

Certainly not all the road trips were like that one. I have vivid memories of many which I enjoyed tremendously. I supposed I got my love of travel from my father, although he always accused my mother of having the travelling bug. He would say, "I am telling you, my children, your mother has eaten '*unyawo yengulube*'". This was an African saying literally meaning "to eat the foot of a pig" and it was used to refer to people who liked going somewhere, or were always ready to go. I think my father liked to travel, but my mother liked going away. He liked to discover new places and meet new people and he would take many photographs to capture those travels. But my father was a strict man and ruled the roost with an iron fist. He was a tall and strong man and he was statuesque. My mother on the other hand was short, the shortest person in our household, spoke softly and I suppose accepted her life as the wife of a harsh man. I think she was resigned to her life and must have realised that in the material world she was better off than any of her family. My father showered her with expensive gifts that made her smile. Her need to go away was perhaps to temper the rage bursts and realities of living under such a regime. As for me I realise now that I inherited both traits from them, although I love to travel and have visited many countries all over the world, like my mother, I go away a lot.

The irony of my father's accusations about my promiscuous lifestyle is that I was extremely under confident and/or uninterested in the areas of romance, love, kissing, boyfriends and sex. About this I knew I was different from many people. My friend Bongi was in a serious relationship and all my friends on campus were sexually active. I would not be surprised if I was the only virgin there.

I have thought about this, and I think much of it had to do with the insatiable appetite I had for finding out what life has to offer, and because I have a natural attraction for things of the brain, I gravitated towards people I thought were interesting and loved to discuss the deeper meaning of life, the politics of the day, alternative economic systems, the future and astrology. Perhaps it was because of my upbringing where I never felt that there was anything special about me on a physical level, or the beatings I received, or the visits from that man at night, or the insults and criticisms from my father. Maybe all of these played a role, but I was not really into those romance things because I did not really feel beautiful or very feminine.

I hardly ever spoke about my home and my family when I was at university. I gave Bongi glimpses of what my life was before that, but could never really get to the point of telling her everything. As I became more socially conscious, I became increasingly embarrassed by my father's wealth. There was not an easy way to discover what I came from, because I did not dress to impress, my father gave me very little money, and I did not speak about it. I got to meet a few black students who had come from means, and it was visible. Mostly these students came from the Bantustans, and were the sons and daughters of heads of the universities there or were in governance structures of these apartheid-formations. The apartheid government had created a pseudo self governing system within the Bantustans or Homelands, as they were called, and these were governed by black people, normally tribe specific. So on the east of the country there was the Transkei and the Ciskei created for the Xhosa people and in the north west part of the country there was Bophuthatswana, meant to govern the Tswana people.

In the first year of university, we were expected to share a room with another student. I entered the on-campus residency five months after university started because the residences were fully booked at the time. I lived with my aunt, my father's youngest sister, and her husband for these months, in a township for mixed race people. I loved my aunt and enjoyed staying with her, although I did not like the area. In the evenings we would knit together, listen to records of Al Green and her husband would play the guitar. But the area was not for me. It was a township where one could see what the neighbours were doing. I was also not street wise and I was different from everyone there, I did not fit in. Many of the people there were very racist and often referred to black people in very derogatory terms. I would take a bus into the city centre every morning and walk across a bridge that joined the city centre to the university area.

After this brief stay with my aunt, I joined Gugu in a room at the end of a fairly long corridor on the sixth floor of one of the three university residences where women could stay. She was the daughter of a fairly prominent family in Bophuthatswana and reportedly powerful in that area. Although university was a great leveller, the status and position of her family was visible. I got on fairly well with Gugu and I liked her a lot. She was studying medicine and spent much time, as did all the medical students, with her books, studying. I was very aware of her need to study and read through those volumes of medical texts and journals, and gave her the space to do that. She was a beautiful woman with smooth dark skin and she was tall. She took great care in her grooming and wore very good quality clothes. Although she had a shy smile, she had an air of confidence about her that could only be accounted for by growing up knowing that you are a class above the rest. Mangope, who was the head of that Bantustan at the time, was renowned for taking care of his people. He built good schools and colleges to educate his people. The area was also relatively well developed with good infrastructure and road network. They also had a media network, complete with their own radio and television station.

On the whole, most people who were from that area felt better off than most other black people, but Gugu was born into the upper echelons of that system, and it showed. There was a classiness about the way she dressed, spoke and generally conducted her business that made you aware that she was some kind of royalty. There was much about her that was different from me. I could not care less about labels and good quality clothes, I did not pay much attention to my physical appearance and I did everything in my power to conceal that my parents were wealthy. She liked doing girly things like applying make-up and would invest her time in manicuring her nails and had very feminine linen. I did not care much for adornments.

But there was something in her that I identified with. She grew up not worrying about what she needed to live on a daily basis and neither did I. We came from means and therefore we were both not really impressed or driven by it, or by the pursuit of it. Although she had access to cash and cars to take her wherever she needed to go, there was an underlying sense that the pursuit of money was not the ultimate goal. It was more about what we were going to do with our lives.

I have since seen clearly how this distinguishes people from each other. Of course, once again a generalisation but I can only speak of my own experiences and observations of myself and those that I encounter. When you grow up not worrying about where money will come from for the basics, there is a peace that you have about provision and about your survival on the basic level. Your panics and fears are not about whether you will make it through the day or week or month or year or in the future. There is a knowing that you get from being born into enough that makes you know, just *sabi*, that you are okay and that you will be just fine tomorrow. The ability to afford things, even though you are not working or wealthy yourself, is never really in doubt. This *sabi* brings with it a certain mentality or belief, even though you had no part in forming it, that life has enough. You see life, even though you may not be conscious of it, as an endless or bottomless place from which all can participate, and that it is through your entrepreneurship, education, hard work, focus and being smart that you can partake of the endlessness that the universe provides. I think the reality that I am and have always been generous beyond what is good for me is based on a *sabi* that life has more to offer. It is also rare for me to be jealous of people; instead I celebrate when people reach new heights, new levels. That usually really excites me and gives me hope. And through my life I have given very many people significant breaks so that they can flourish. I saw my father do this all the time, and I just became that way. Gugu and I had this in common, and even though many of my friends at university who did not come from this could not understand why we got along or why we liked each other, this was something we shared. So very few of our conversations or interactions were based on lack or desperation.

I have found over the years that people we encounter are indeed mirrors of who we are, or at least of what we believe. She reflected that part of me, of what I came from, and what I was as a result of what I came from. She did not share with me the beatings,

146

torture and having to fend for myself from an early age, neither did she share with me the feeling of not being okay, at least not within her family structure. In her family, they all looked the same and therefore self acceptance was a given, at least in the family setting. And it showed. She was more confident than I was about who she was and never really made comments suggesting differently. I admired that about her.

But she struggled academically, and when I moved on to my second year, she had to write a motivation, supported by her parents, on why she should not be excluded from returning to the university the following year. In my second year, she repeated her first year. I had much empathy for her situation, because she worked hard to achieve her pass, but it was tough for her. I did not really think that that is what she was supposed to do with her life, although she said it was what she wanted. I had a feeling, a strong one, that it was to live up to the requirements of what she came from. In this way I was fortunate, because my parents were not noted for their academic pursuits; whatever I did academically actually set the benchmark for others to follow. So even the move from law to arts would probably never have happened in that family.

Is it possible that some things you go through or are exposed to, no matter how bad it feels at the time, are what you need for where you are going? Or could it be that the circumstances you go through determine what you become or where you go to?

I began to define some of who I was when I was at university. It was a long time since I did not feel negative about my hair, although Gugu often said she wished she had hair like mine. I could not believe that there were people who thought I had good hair. I was at the bottom of the rung where I came from, and here at the university a woman who grew up feeling good about who she was, and had an air of confidence about her, longed to have hair like mine. The reality is that we had the same hair. Life is strange, and as I have come to realise, everything is relative.

I have very distinct memories about my hair from when I was growing up. The first thing I remember is how my mother braided my hair. There were two hairstyles that she made which made both of us very happy. She would make a side path from my forehead to the crown of my head, and then another from that point to the right ear. That would form the first part and she would braid it and put a ribbon or bonbon at the end of it. Then she would divide the rest of my hair into two by making a path from the midpoint of my crown to the neck, and would braid each of these sections. I loved this hairstyle, especially when my mother made it. My mother never made a single negative comment about my hair, not once. I think she really liked my hair and loved combing it. Maybe because I was the only daughter with this kind of hair and it was a novel thing for her. The other hairstyle she made, my mother would divide my hair into two parts from ear to ear and would put an elastic band on each part, braid the parts that were "free" and put a bonbon where the braid ended. When she washed my hair, before she tamed it with braids, it would stand in a very big afro, and the longer my hair grew, the more the afro drooped. She would look at me and smile and call me Joan Armatrading. I liked Ms Armatrading before I knew her music.

When I lived with my paternal grandmother for the first years of my schooling, she or her helper would comb my hair and both appeared to enjoy combing it. My sister however did not have such a good time. She

148

was very scared of a comb because like me she had very sensitive scalp, but she hated the combing process and would cry loudly, pleading for mercy when her hair was combed. She had silky hair so I could not really understand why she made such a fuss about it, it just appeared much easier to work with than mine, which knotted very easily.

My first bad experience with my hair came when my maternal grandmother visited our house and stayed for quite a while. I could not wait for her to leave. She would comb my hair and take out on it her obvious disappointment that my mother had married my father. I did not know up until that point that my maternal grandparents were not happy with this union of my parents. She would comb my hair aggressively and each stroke would be accompanied by comments relating to my coarse hair and blaming my father for its coarseness. She would make many comments about my mother being stupid for marrying that man and for producing a kid that had this kind of hair. I do not ever remember liking this grandmother. What I remember is the mole on her face, the very long black and white hair and that I never really saw her smile. I can't even imagine laughter in her presence, from her or anybody else.

Not all of my mother's family were like that, though; there were some who were very different. I liked her youngest sister and her daughter very much, and a few of her brother's children, as well as one of her brothers, who liked to call me "Tea" because I liked tea so much. I still do. There is nothing quite like a well made cup of tea.

My second and worst experience of knowing there was something wrong with my hair came from Cruella of Harding. By the time I went to that place I had really long hair, and I was able to wash, comb out and braid it myself. But this woman saw my hair and said I had to do something about "that bush on your head". The word "kroes" was used to describe hair like mine, and I heard it often. She told me I had to relax my hair, because I could not be going around with that kind of hair. She bought straightener with the money my father would leave for her to buy things when we needed them, and proceeded to straighten my hair. At the end of that process I had hair that looked much like my sister's and I was shocked by how long it actually was; because the curl had been removed from it, it just lay down flat, like my maternal grandmother's or my sister's hair flowed. She also cut about half of it off, and commented that it was too long for me to take care of properly. That process for me was very humiliating. My hair, although undesirable to her and my maternal grandmother, differentiated me from my sister; now there was not much difference, except for the skin of course. I hated her in that moment more than any other, and the act of cutting it off I felt even at that age was beyond nastiness, it was jealousy. People tend to have an obsession about long hair in this community.

When I went to boarding school, I kept this relaxed hair and learnt how to take care of relaxed hair from other girls. There was much "kroes" calling at that school, but none of it bothered me more than I had already been bothered about it before. The girls would wash their hair weekly at the boarding house although those with relaxed hair would wash it less often, perhaps every two weeks, because you needed to allow oil build-up, as the relaxer removed all the natural moisturisers from your hair. The washing process would be followed by conditioning to help retain some moisture. I learnt that you needed to put a plastic bag over your hair and wait about twenty minutes to condition the hair properly. After this it was customary to put curlers into the hair and wait in the sun for the hair to dry. The older girls inducted the younger girls into how to do this process properly so that the kroes hairs, where there was new growth, did not show.

The idea was to make all the hair look silky and smooth, and not reveal the natural hair. After the hair was dry, you had to apply oil on the hair and then "swirl" it. Swirling was meant to straighten the hair out further and keep the natural hair under control. It involved making a path from ear to ear, just like my mother did when I was younger, and then combing it from one side to the other until all the hair was joined together and swirling around the head. You were then required to put a piece of a pantyhose that was cut from an old pair over the head, and to turn it until it was flat against the head. When you removed the pantyhose more than an hour later, the hair would be flowing on your head the same way it would on my mother's head. That was the ultimate hairstyle for Coloured people. With this hair you also had to be careful not to go into the rain, because then it would change. Moisture from the rain, from being splashed when you were sitting near the pool or from sweatiness from playing sport spoilt things. Your mission was to keep the hair dry, put oils on it at night and swirl it each night. The process of the hair changing was called "going home". So when it rained, you would hear many girls screaming, "Ah no, the damn rain, where is the umbrella, my hair is going to go home". Or the older girls would advise you to make sure that you put Amla Oil on your hair before you swirl it to prevent it from "going home".

When I came to university, I decided I had had enough of relaxing and fearing for my hair going home, and decided to let it live at home. This protracted process of hair preparation and fearing for its return to its natural state also created endless comedies in my world. Another motivation was that I really did not like spending so much of my time on my hair. I felt it was a waste of time as it took up more time than the value it provided me. Even at this stage I was doing cost benefit analyses! I would later be more conscious of how much I revered time and how it was spent.

My decision to end this inanity of hair care would be another step in my transformative process. I went to the local barber on Jorissen Street and asked them to cut my hair off...all of it. The guy who was there was Coloured and tried to change my mind, pointing out that it would take a long time to grow it back. The truth is that my hair, since it was subjected to chemicals, never grew back as long as it did when it was natural, because those chemicals really do rob the hair of many things, and it weakens it, and the longer it gets, the uglier the ends look. It also breaks if you put too much chemical on it, and many have to keep trimming it to keep it looking good. I had made up my mind and nothing was going to change it, and I left that barber that day with a brush cut, feeling really good about taking control back of my hair and image.

My family reacted with horror to this new hairstyle of mine, but I enjoyed this new freedom of not having to take care of my hair with such routine, and I felt I was taking a stand for who I was in my natural state. I wore large earrings with my brush cut hair and liked the look a lot. But my hair grows quite fast, and soon I had an afro. I left that afro to grow really long, and looked like Roberta Flack did on the photographs of her *Quiet Fire* and *First Take* albums. I liked this look even better. Sometimes I would have my hair braided in cornrows, much like the musician d'Angelo in his very sensuous rendition of *Cruisin'* or *Send it On*. Sometimes I would just comb it back and put on an

Alice-band to hold the hair back, then I looked much like Jill Scott does when she keeps her hair in its natural state. I did not get any compliments from my family, but my mother liked the afro and told me I really had the Joan Armatrading look.

This look fitted in very well with my general lifestyle on campus, but more particularly with my other passion which was starting to find expression. I had met quite a few students who loved music and would join them in their jam sessions. I would not sing, but I would sit with them and do much singing along in my head. Some of the students, one who has since became world renowned for jazz, were studying music at the university. I was pleased to see that people could actually study music full time, and they had dreams and plans of doing music as a career when they left the university. I attended many of these sessions without participating and would tell all that I could not sing.

I was not at all confident about my musical ability or talent. I had loved singing and music since I was very young, and it always stirred something indescribable inside of me. Music helped me to cry and it soothed me too. It also facilitated my travel into the other world that I had created, and I find to this day that music makes me know that there is a God. I grew up around music, my father could sing, and his sister had a powerful voice, singing often in church, with no need for a microphone. When we were younger, my aunt would perform at gigs in what was known as Lorenzo Marques in Mozambique, which we visited often.

Within my home my father required all of us to sing. To this present day, when my siblings and I get together and reminisce about my father's stories, growing up or "those days", one of us will start singing and, without provocation, everyone will join in. We will never forget the lyrics of those songs because we had to sing those songs of my father's choosing over and over again. When we travelled we were expected to sing, and we did not complain, because in the heart of us all, the love of music is ingrained. The only time this became a problem was when we were travelling, and my father wanted us to sing when we were exhausted and as a result we would fall asleep in the car. I would be often woken up with the sting from the back of my father's hand against my cheek. Then it was not so pleasant to be singing.

My mother played the piano and she also loved to sing. All of us had a deeper textured voice than my mother did. Hers was beautiful, light and very Celtic in texture. My voice was not as deep and loud as my aunt who did not require a microphone, neither was it as light and crispy as my mother's; it resided somewhere between the two. When I was much younger, whenever I sang, I was asked to turn down the volume, and I began to sing very softly. But my mom would often play the piano and ask me to sing. Normally it was renditions of songs from the Shirley Bassey and Perry Como albums or gospel music mainly from Jimmy Swaggart albums. But my mother also loved Miriam Makeba and we would often do renditions of her songs. During the December holidays, my mother would play many of the Christmas carols on the piano and the entire family would sing along. Music was central to our lives growing up.

I attended these jam sessions at university and was really afraid of singing in public. I was to meet someone who would change that completely and would eventually make me believe that a career in music was more than possible. I had met him before in very unusual circumstances. I was walking from the university lecture halls towards the residence one afternoon when I met my friend Ricky, who was the

154

one who had been asking me on a date for a while. My new found freedom and growing joy meant that I was smiling a lot and generally feeling on top of the world. When Ricky and I met, we exchanged cheek kisses and he introduced me to his friend. I put out my hand to greet him, and he said, "What are you smiling at? Do you really go around smiling like that?" and also said something about do I think the world is so great. I was stunned and ill prepared for that comment. Without saying a word I kept on walking towards the residence. Ricky ran after me and told me not to be affected by what had happened and that his friend could not have meant what he said. I was not interested, and continued to my room.

When I got into the room I started frothing at the mouth, pacing up and down my room. Who does he think he is? How can he talk to me like that? Does he think I am his damn punching bag? If he has a problem with the world, why take it out on me? And what is wrong with smiling anyway? If he can't smile, well now, that is his business and certainly not mine! How could Ricky expose me to that rude thing? The next time I see him I will tell him what's on my mind! He will hear from me! I hate him!

The next few times I met him I was engulfed by a hatred for Ricky's friend. He did apologise and said that he had just been joking, but I was not to believe that. He took the wind out of my sails and I did not have time for him. But Ricky and I were very close and so I got to see his friend quite often. We would often meet at Ricky's flat, which was outside of the campus, on Jorissen Street. We had many fun nights there because Ricky knew many people and often we would go there, he would cook and we would have long nights discussing politics and other trivial issues. The tension between us subsided somewhat through these meetings at Ricky's place, but there remained an underlying current which was tense and I could not figure out why there was such a negative and disturbing current between us.

One afternoon I was at the jam session and singing in my head along with the live and wondrous sounds of the acoustic arrangements. One of the guys, who was later to become a famous actor in the South African movie, soapie and theatrical scene, said that a friend of his would be joining to play the piano. The students were in full swing trying new sounds when in walks this man, smiling! Every part of my being was egging me on to ask "Why are you smiling?" but I resisted. He was introduced to all the other musicians there, and when it came to his introduction to me..."I know him", I quickly said. The band members asked how, and I responded before his dumb mouth would put a foot in it, "He is a friend of a friend". He just smiled and walked to the piano. I was to be silenced.

The sounds that came out of that room that afternoon will not leave my memory, ever. As he was playing, I just saw him in a different light, he looked different, and I could swear that there was something shining from his face when he started to play that piano. There was a part of me that felt that he was born to play the piano, for me. I cannot explain it, the touch on the keys and the way he lifted his fingers off the keys were different, and I understood what he was trying to convey through that instrument, way down deep in my soul. I cannot look at singer songwriter John Legend without thinking of this man, not only do they have very similar looks, there is just a way about him that reminds me of this pianist who was Ricky's friend. Just to make sure that I kept my cool, I escaped into my world and in it I smiled from ear to ear and let out a small yepee!

I came back into this world, when I was aware of my name being called. "Hello! Hello there!...What are you doing here? Do you play an instrument? Are you an instrument?" he said, smirking. One of the band members said, "No she is just a fan and a friend". I stood up from where I was sitting on the floor, and with no thought in my mind and no action planned, I walked straight to the piano, looked him squarely in the eyes and asked, "Do you know *The greatest love of all*?" He didn't respond but just started playing it, and I started to sing as if my life did not exist before then. I never once thought about anything, I just sang. When the song was finished I asked, once again looking straight into his face, and said "Malaika"; once again he just started playing. I missed the intro, because that caught me off guard, I had assumed that he would not know it. That was one of my mother's favourite songs, sung by Miriam Makeba and Harry Belafonte. But I quickly caught up and sang the song. Silence again, then he asked, "Do you know any Shirley Bassey?" And then I broke inside and said "No". He said, "That's a pity, I really like her music and I think you would sound great singing her songs."

Then the reality of everything that had just happened struck me like a thunderbolt and I felt sick to my stomach. Everyone started gathering around me. "Girl, you have been here all these months with a voice like that! Why did you never sing? You should sing in our band! Wow, girl, you sound amazing!"

I was not prepared and ready for the well of emotions inside of me. I held myself together like a taut rope that could snap at any moment under the strain of the moment, and said softly, "I am late for my study group." I picked up my bag and I left, unceremoniously. I rushed back to my room at the residence and I cried me a river. I cried for a very long time, not even sure why I was crying, but it was my soul that was crying and I had no control of it. I cried myself to sleep that day.

I woke up feeling strange though light, but also confused and resigned at the same time. As quickly and as suddenly as those feelings and the need to cry came, they were gone. I went to lectures as usual, actually read my notes after lectures and got very busy with my assignments, which I was behind with. I spent much time in my room after that and my lecturers were happy. I submitted all outstanding assignments including those that were not yet due. I was extremely productive at the time. I did not listen to music in that week-long period, I was very focused and reminded myself that I was there to get a degree. I spent much of my time reading the suggested materials, reading my notes and getting to understand those concepts on a different level. I also spring cleaned my room and filed my notes into easily accessible files and overall was very proud about how my room looked. At the time I was doing this, I questioned my approach to studies, and thought that I should perhaps begin to focus more on my course work. I began to philosophise about how fortunate I was to be there and that I had not really taken this opportunity as seriously as I should have. I ignored all notes placed under my door, as well as the knocking on my door. I was emotionless, focused, determined and highly productive.

This resolution was not to last. The cracks started to appear after an interesting Industrial Sociology lecture by Professor Eddie Webster, about "deskilling the labour force", when I found Ricky waiting for me at the exit of the hall. I short circuited all his questions regarding my whereabouts by telling him that I was not well and took time off to recover. He did not believe me but surmised that he should leave it there, and asked if I was feeling better. I responded in the affirmative, but also told him that I needed time to rest. He agreed that I should rest, but asked me to first have lunch at his place. We walked to his flat together and he in his typical style made dry jokes which made me laugh for most of the walk there. Ricky always had a way of converting my simpers into a full-blown laugh. By the time we got there I was laughing, but it was soon to be replaced with simpering.

When we reached his building the pianist was there and the simpering returned with a vengeance. Ricky told the pianist that I had not been well in the past week. The pianist said he hoped I was feeling better and it was good to see me again. I spent the rest of the afternoon in that flat with the three of us talking about all sorts of things, except what had happened in the music session. I was pleased that he did not raise the incident and I treated the pianist like a stranger I had just met. This was the first time we actually spoke directly to each other and our friendship developed from that moment.

I did not go to the music group for another week but would visit Ricky's flat daily and the three of us became very close during that period. The pianist asked many questions about where I was from, my family and what I wanted to do after university. I replied by giving very little information, but enough to keep the conversation and friendship going. He intimated that he was not enjoying his studies at university, and if he had it his way he would leave university. Both Ricky and I implored him to do what was necessary to finish his degree, pointing out that he could get a good job if he had an engineering degree. But there was a look in his eye which showed that nothing we said was getting through. He had made up his mind, although he was not saying that. That time was characterised by lots of debates and laughing. One evening we chatted until midnight and we all agreed to crash at Ricky's place for the rest of the night. The next morning Ricky made French toast for breakfast before we went to our respective lectures. Ricky was studying and working at the same time, so he had access to money, a rarity for me and most students.

The three of us became very close and this friendship was to go on after I had finished with university, and both were to be very influential in my life, and impact it in ways that I did not imagine at the time. We had agreed sometime during the week to go to movies in Mayfair on the Saturday and Ricky was to treat us to curries for lunch. Mayfair was a commercial and residential place in Johannesburg where Asian people lived. It also housed the Oriental Plaza, which is a really large retail centre wherein many Indian traders sold their wares at affordable prizes. That Saturday, Ricky and I walked down to the movies together and we met the pianist there. We watched the first movie, one I cannot recall, and then went to have lunch together at the Oriental Plaza. While dining, Ricky said that he wanted to watch an alternatively-rated movie later that afternoon and asked us to join him. He felt I was rather innocent and naive, and needed to be exposed to real life. I almost choked on the bunny chow I was eating. A bunny, as it was called, is a quarter loaf of bread with the soft inside removed and replaced with curry. After much persuasion I agreed to join my friends for my first alternative movie. What I will say about that movie is that it was not of very good quality. The sound and picture quality left much to be desired.

The pianist, who had a Mini car at the time, said he would drive us back home. We argued at length about who should be dropped off first, reached no resolution and agreed to crash at Ricky's place again. We played cards and other silly games until the early hours of the morning. Two of Ricky's friends joined us during the course of the night, with wine and snacks. We all pushed the boundaries that night. We played "spin the bottle", a game where a bottle of wine is spun and whomever the neck of the bottle faces when it stops spinning has to either remove an item of clothing or do something that the previous victim commanded. We spent at least half an hour debating the rules of the game, but eventually agreed.

The bottle first landed in Zodwa's direction, one of the two women who had joined in the course of the night. She removed her denim jacket. For some reason that bottle did not land in my direction for a very long time and no one was very happy with that. Ricky tried to introduce a new rule to change this, but both the pianist and I disagreed. However, my fortunes did soon change, and soon I was removing items of clothing. I was dared to give Angeline a French kiss, which I did. The rule was that you could choose whether you would take off clothes or do a dare, but if you were naked you had to do a dare. I alternated these two to give myself a fair chance of not having to play the rest of the game naked. By the end of the night there were five very tipsy naked people. The first rule we agreed to was that there would be no sexual activity and we were all bound to that agreement. So that is where things ended.

After that day the friendship between us grew. We had removed the unspoken boundaries and there was little left to fear about each other. I was growing up fast, but still did not have the desire to have a boyfriend. This situation was ideal for me. I had an amazing friendship with guys and could call on them to do the movie thing or just chill without all the hassles I witnessed the women on campus go through. The arrangement was nearly derailed when Ricky wanted the three of us to swear not to make moves on each other. He told the pianist that he had tried and failed with me and he was okay with it, as long as the pianist and I did not do anything romantic. I immediately agreed but the pianist protested. This put a strain on our arrangement for some time. But we soon overcame it as I assured both of them that I was unlikely to do anything with either of them.

I returned to the music group during this intense period and began to sing with the group. I was able to sing in rehearsals but still had some reservations about my range, and the pianist noticed that I sang under my breath when there were notes I was not sure of. My confidence, however, did grow and I began to spend much of my time singing with the group. I had never performed a lead in a band in public, except in church, but then I was always with my sister and I had felt safe in those circumstances. The band performed in various small bars, venues and student events. This was a good time for me, I was singing and feeling good about it. Most of the performances were jazz, and I performed some of the Ella Fitzgerald, Dolly Radebe, Miriam Makeba, Nina Simone and Thandi Klaasen songs. I loved, and hated Nina Simone. I loved her music very much and especially how her emotions were conveyed through the piano and through her voice. But I hated her too because her songs reflected what I was and felt inside of me. Sometimes when I listened to her songs I would feel very bad and that torrent inside me would grow and I did not know what to do about it. It often caused me to take a razor to smooth the areas under my feet. In these times that pressure from within would subside. Our guitarist wrote a few songs for me to perform, and I felt good that there were songs written especially for me. During that period I began to feel that this was what I wanted to do with my life.

After I graduated with the Bachelor's degree, Ricky suggested that I consider enrolling in a Master's programme which he had been accepted for. I applied, went for the interviews and was accepted. My father had stopped paying for my tuition, as I had successfully applied for a student loan. The programme had around ten post graduate students and was a healthy mix of races, ages and backgrounds. I revelled in this learning environment. It was not easy to shake off my minimalist-study approach because it allowed me time to do the music, participate in political activities, continue organising social events for black students and have long evenings with Ricky and the pianist. But this course was more intense and perhaps for the first time I felt I was really challenged. The lecturers were passionate about the subject matter and it rubbed off on me. I learnt many things on that course and it helped to provide a structure that brought together my natural talent for thinking ahead and planning, with my growing need to work in areas that could actually make a difference.

The course was also the most practical learning I had done to that date. It was gratifying to visit different areas where we could see the impact of the apartheid planning policies we were reading about. The lecturers were also relatively progressive and managed to link the political, economic and social policies of apartheid to the spatial realities in how urban and rural areas were being formed, or under developed. We explored the impact of how apartheid spatial planning resulted in the formation of townships and what it meant for rural areas, as well as the economic cost to the country of this political philosophy of separate development. It cost the country dearly. The time that commuters spent on the road in the name of keeping black people separate was too long and this had a significant economic cost for the country as a whole.

We were challenged to read about other spatial planning models around the world, and link them to those specific political, economic and social realities, and I enjoyed researching these various models. We were also challenged as the possible future leaders of the country on what we would do to ensure economic and social development in the country. It was a challenge, because the spatial realities of South Africa could not just be changed; houses could not be moved at will, and the infrastructure that held South Africa together was built firstly to achieve separate development before any economic and social imperatives. I got to see how the folly of an atrocious political system had really handcuffed the planners of the future to some extent. I learnt about transport economics and the key role a robust transportation network played in the development of a country. This interested me significantly because my father was also in the freighting business and I understood how the movement of people and goods was linked to creating future economic possibilities.

Asinine beliefs, based on race, create asinine spatial models. I wondered how the apartheid system spatial planners ignored the logical approaches to development in favour of an illogical one. Perhaps ideology was too powerful, and logic took a backseat.

Ricky and I began spending much more time together because we would debate these issues in depth and challenge each other on what was possible. We both were getting increasingly irritated by the conclusions we were often reaching. We were discussing these things within the framework of an apartheid regime; how could any of these matter now? We concluded that our insights and skills were not

164

useful to this kind of South Africa, and that it needed to be free for us to really make an impact. We realised that we could never work for the various institutions that would need planners, because we could in effect be participating in upholding a system that we knew was designed for an ideology that was fundamentally flawed and unjust.

During this course, I met a man who I got to like a lot. I liked the way his mind worked and I liked the way he commanded himself. I really liked him, and we got along well. He was from the Eastern Cape and he had a way of speaking that drew me to him. I caught myself watching him a few times, and wondered what would happen if I just told him that I thought he was okay. But I did not, and a few times he gave me compliments that made me blush. So in those two years of this course I watched him, and he made compliments and that is where it stayed. We shared political viewpoints about many things, although my own leanings were more to the left than his. Towards the end of the first year of this course he was to go home and when he returned he was a different person. He walked differently and he spoke as if he was ten years older than before. There was also a calm about him that made him so much more attractive to me. "I have been to the mountain," he said when I asked why he looked so different. "I have become a man!" Later he was to leave for Harvard, where he continued his studies.

The pianist did not finish his degree, but we were not surprised. He was extremely bored with his studies and did not want to be at university. I had moved into a flat outside the campus area, and was doing part time jobs to help pay my way. My student loan was not enough to cover my needs. I was extremely grateful that my father had sent me to a typing course when I was in my first year of university. That skill of being able to do touch typing really helped me in my life as a whole, and my father must have known that I was meant to write. And in the past two years it had helped me survive, because I was able to type my assignments, but it became a source of income for me. Many of the students got to know that I could type, really fast, and began to give me their handwritten assignments and projects to type. I got most of my work from post graduate students who needed typing and layout services for their project and their theses. I had also helped some of the wealthier students who needed ironing services. Many students did not like to iron their clothes, and that provided some extra cash for me. I also found some part time employment in the non-governmental organisations. I relished this environment, of civil society, because I felt that this is where people who wanted to make a difference and change things could find a home.

The three of us continued to meet, in my or Ricky's flat, as well as a flat that the pianist had moved into, in Hillbrow. This was a very good time for the three of us; we were all involved in some kind of work and had some spare money between us. We would go out together to clubs at night, and we began to eat at restaurants more often. We were enjoying our lives, but often it would be interrupted by the violence and anger around us.

One night the three of us were getting ready to leave a club at night when we heard shooting outside. A man had left the club and was followed outside by another, who fired shots and killed him. The reason the shooter killed the victim was because he thought that he had given too much attention to the shooter's girlfriend when he was in the club. It is indeed sad that he, like many of us, have not found other means of resolving conflict, or other means to stymie that volcanic pressure of rage that is inside us. Perhaps we have to first acknowledge that we are an angry nation.

The reality is that the shooter was arrested by police but did not get convicted for the crime, because his docket mysteriously disappeared from the police. Later on in my life I would be aware of an employee who shot his girlfriend. Everyone knew he had shot her, but weeks later he reported for work. He boasted to some of us that "anyone can make a docket disappear". Perhaps it is very difficult to change a culture of femicide or violent crimes, unless there are consequences. If people think they can get away with it, maybe it is just easier to reach for that gun.

At the end of the first year of the Master's programme, I failed to hand in an assignment on time; in fact I slipped it under her door on the day it was due, but later on in the afternoon. The lecturer responsible for that course refused to accept that assignment, and decided to give me a *Not Completed* result. For some reason she reminded me of my maternal grandmother. I think it is the way she used to look at me. That decision would affect me negatively. I spoke to the course organiser, whom I liked very much, about what my options were. He agreed to speak to her, but was not successful in convincing her to grade my assignment. In the end my options were spelt clearly for me – I could not move onto my fifth and final year of studies until I completed that course. He agreed, however, that I could begin the thesis part of the second year, and would need to spend another six months on the course work the year after that. I agreed with this option, although I was irritated with the situation. Whilst I take responsibility for handing in the assignment late on that day, I did not believe that the punishment fitted the crime. It was a disproportionate response.

Labour

I entered the fifth year of university with much less enthusiasm than I had the year before, but nevertheless continued. One evening Ricky, the pianist and I were cooking together in the Hillbrow flat and I told them that I wanted to start looking for a job. The pianist said that he was aware of an internal advertisement in the human resources department where he worked and that he would bring it for me. The three of us later filled in that application form, and within two weeks I was employed, after attending an interview. It was my first interview for a job, and although Ricky and the pianist were quite nervous for me, I did not have any fear. Maybe it is because I did not really want to do it and was conflicted about whether to take on a full time job or continue to do part time jobs, so I could complete the course. But when I went for the interview my desire to win took over and the Human Resource Manager commented that I had a very good interview.

That was a very different world for me and the job did not provide much of a challenge. This was a large company, listed on the Johannesburg Stock Exchange, and there were many employees. I was responsible for assisting with personnel policies, particularly those to do with industrial relations. This was not my thing. I had my own office, was being paid a competitive salary and could afford many things I could not before. I could pay for my accommodation, new clothes and could contribute substantially to the social budget of the three of us. And from my very first pay cheque, I was able to send money to my parents and buy them things that they liked, which made me very happy. I did not like this job, and felt that what I had learnt in the formal and informal education in the campus years had gone to waste. In my second week of working there, I put on my wall a very large poster of Ruud Gullit, a black Dutch football player who had won the best footballer of the year award. I was the only black person in that department and people really did not know what to say when they came into my office. On the poster it read "This award is dedicated to Nelson Mandela". I did not need to say anything, that poster spoke for me before I opened my mouth.

The pianist and I would spend most of our lunch breaks together at the canteen, which was substantially sponsored for employees. It was the first time that he and I had a relationship outside of the music, which had lessened by that time, apart from with Ricky. Up until that point Ricky was the glue that held us all together and the common denominator, as he had initially been a friend of both of us. The pianist was driving a car that his mother had loaned him to get to work, and we would travel to and from work every day together. Our friendship deepened and we started realising how alike we really were. We both liked alone time and loved talking and discussing concepts until we had exhausted the topic. He had a very high level of intelligence which I marvelled at. He was also not easily impressed by glitter and sizzle, he was far more interested in the steak, the substance. So we got along very well.

We began discussing the jobs we were in and we both felt that they were inconsequential to our lives. We nevertheless got to keep working in that company and would spend much of our time together. Some lunch times we would drive together to the nearby town to have lunch or I would accompany him to choose linen or other items for his apartment. Our trips to and from work and our lunch times together we both looked forward to.

This was to change somewhat before we both left. It was a Saturday morning that I went to the pianist's apartment in Hillbrow to visit, as I would often do. When I got there, he was not alone. There was a woman there sitting in the lounge. I greeted her and went to his room. He told me he had gone out the previous night, got really drunk and the woman in the lounge had stayed over. He still had a hangover from the previous night. I laughed, but he did not laugh with me; perhaps it was the headache he was nursing, but probably it was because he was feeling embarrassed. He was very particular about his space, and who stayed over. I told him I was going to make breakfast and he joined me in the kitchen. His brother arrived while we were making breakfast and the three of us, with the woman, ate brunch together. I went to sit on the balcony to have a cigarette, a habit I regrettably picked up from Ricky in the third year of university, and the pianist joined me, asking how he could get the woman to leave. He did not have to explain because I had got to know him very well by that time, and like me he liked being alone. We agreed that we would announce that he was taking me to the East Rand to visit my brother who was staying there at the time. He briefed his brother about the plan, and it worked. I took my jacket, and he took the keys of the car and told the woman that we were leaving. She then also left.

We did get into the car but travelled instead to the south of Johannesburg where his folks lived. I had been there before. The pianist would often take Ricky and me to his house and we had many lunches and dinners with his folks. He had a sister, younger than he was, who was still at high school. She reminded me of myself and I did not really know why at the time. His mother was an amazing cook and I once watched her make a steak and kidney pie from scratch. His parents were very welcoming to his friends. We spent some time there before his headache got the better of him, and we headed back to Hillbrow. What we both did not know was that day and his indiscretions on the previous night would impact him in the future. A few months later he would find out that the woman was pregnant, and this was something that he certainly had not planned for.

We would go to jazz clubs at least twice a week. Sometimes the pianist joined the musicians who were performing. Music was his first love and he came alive when he was playing that piano. We got to watch very young musicians who later got to make a name for themselves in the post apartheid era. Our lives were full and busy. We had jobs, and although we were not happy with them, they provided more than enough funding for us to have a good life and feed our need for jazz clubs, making music and travelling.

During this time, the lease on my flat expired, and I decided to move to downtown Johannesburg where the pianist had located a three bedroom flat that could accommodate me and my two younger brothers. The apartment was in Jeppe Street, and very centrally located near the bus and taxi ranks. The brother immediately after me was to enrol in a technical college and the youngest was to complete high school on the West Rand. The pianist would visit me in Jeppe Street as usual and one night he parked the car outside the building and came into the flat for a visit, where we listened to jazz and soul records. We decided to go to *Jameson's*, which was a buzzing jazz club not far from where my apartment was located. When we got onto the front balcony, which was also the exit to the apartment, we noticed the familiar orange Ford being driven away. We hurried down to the street but it was too late, the car had been stolen. It was his mother's car and he contemplated for some time how he would tell her. What that meant was that our transport to work was gone and we had to navigate the taxi system to and from work. From then I would take a minibus taxi to Hillbrow, where I would meet him and then we would board another to work together. It was inconvenient, but minibus taxis were readily available.

One afternoon we were travelling back from work together on the minibus taxi when the driver began to fight with one of the passengers. He lost control of the taxi and we had an accident that shook my foundations. A few people were injured but one of the women passengers on board died. The taxi driver, instead of worrying about his passengers, kept fighting with the man he had been fighting before. After that incident I told the pianist that I had to get a car, soon. The reality is that I did not grow up in a township, I was not street wise and felt quite intimidated by those taxis. Also, I had been driving since I was ten and felt better if I was driving. That accident and the circumstances surrounding it really frightened me, and I needed to get a car so as to be more in control of my movements and my future.

My youngest brother was not coping with the freedom of living in Johannesburg and my father decided to send him to a school in Natal. My sister and her husband were living there and he stayed with them. This left the other brother and myself in the flat but he too was not faring well at the technical college. During his stay with me, my brother met and fell head over heels in love with Michelle. She was an attractive woman two years older than I was who had a young baby. My brother was in love with her and would have done anything for her. I joined him one day when he met her at the movies. I liked her from the moment we met and we became very close friends. She loved Peter

Tosh and I loved Bob Marley. I had a particular affinity with *Redemption Song*, and liked that other black people were singing about the things that we were exposed to. I had loved reggae since I was a child, and I got to know of Bob Marley through my father, who loved the song *Chances Are*.

One evening she invited us for dinner at her flat, where she was living with her brother. When we got there I met her brother, whom I thought was rather charming. He had a way about him which intrigued me. I was attracted to him and she later told me that he asked about me quite a lot. But he was seeing another woman, whom Michelle hated with a passion, and she would wish that he could leave her and start seeing me. But it was not to be, I did not like messy situations when it came to romantic matters, and I was not really confident about matters of the heart, although we did get to share a kiss one afternoon. Years later my dear friend would be brutally raped by a family member and lose all grip on reality. Most violent crimes against women in South Africa are perpetrated by people who are known to them, mainly family members. It was very sad for me to see a young beautiful woman so full of life and possibilities being broken in that way.

When my brother dropped out of college he left Johannesburg and I was forced to give up the flat, which was too big for me to live in alone. I also did not feel safe in that area. I often saw and heard instances of domestic violence in those apartments and couldn't stand being reminded of that life. My eldest brother had since married his girlfriend and we agreed that I would stay with them in the East Rand for a while. They lived in a township where Coloured people lived and that environment was very foreign to me. It was not a very good place to raise children. There was much anger in that place, and gangs were the norm. Young girls would be enticed by the "power" and money of those who were in gangs, and teenage pregnancy was a common phenomenon in places like these. It was not uncommon to see young girls out of school with bruises on their faces, scars on their bodies and babies on their arms.

My brother and his wife, whom I liked very much, lived in the flats there at the time and had since had other children. He was struggling with work and she was not working because my brother did not believe that his wife should work. But at this time I was working, getting much more money than I needed and my staying there helped to feed and clothe all of us as well as his children. But I knew that I was not meant to and neither was I equipped to stay in that place. I did not fit in here. David, who was now an in-law, and I began to spend some time together, but he was seeing someone else at the time. When she got to hear of our friendship she was angry, and there was much name calling.

In this place I got to learn of many words that people used for people who looked like me. My hair was in braids at that stage of my life, and I was probably the only one wearing my hair like that in this area. *Kaffir drolletjies* was the term this woman and others used to describe my hair – not very complimentary, I might add. When you take a group of people who are disenfranchised but try to feel superior and put them together in an area, there is much ugliness that comes from their mouths and, no, it does not feel good. But at the same time it is very sad to see people who can barely finish school feel that they are better than you because of hair!

During one Christmas holiday I discussed with my father my need to buy a car. I had since got my driver's licence and was ready to own a car. I discussed various options with my father, and I had identified a Mini that

174

I wanted to buy, but it needed some additional mechanical work. My father said that he would fix the car for me and in the meantime offered that I could take one of his cars and use it until my Mini car was fixed. On my return to Johannesburg, I drove straight to Hillbrow to visit my friend the pianist and to show him the car I would be using. He was very excited for me and we drove around Hillbrow celebrating access to a car again. He told me that his friend Thabiso, who also worked with us as a chemical engineer, was having a New Year's party at his flat. We parked the car at his place and walked to Thabiso's apartment. The party was electrifying when we got there. We partied and I got to meet a few new faces. I met a couple who told me that they had booked a chalet at Ifafa Beach in Natal, but they had no transport to get there as his car had broken down. I was feeling alive and possible at the time and I announced: "I am driving down to Ifafa beach in Natal tomorrow, I need one person to join us?"

On the road back to Johannesburg after visiting my folks, I stopped at a filling station and bought *Cosmopolitan* magazine. I checked my astrological readings and I loved what it said. It stated that this was the year to do something outrageous and that I would have much opportunity to dare to live and spread my wings. It advised to go for it. It is in this spirit that I uttered those words and was willing to begin immediately to spread my wings and dare to live.

The pianist looked at me, very confused, and asked what I was up to. This tall guy whom I had noticed the moment I entered the party said, "I will." I asked him if he was serious and he said "absolutely". We agreed that we would leave the next day at nine o'clock in the morning. I asked the pianist if I could crash at his place, because I did not want to return to the East Rand where I was living with my brother, as I already had a suitcase in the car. But before we went back to his place I danced for hours, mainly with the tall guy who had caught my eye.

When we returned to the pianist's apartment he castigated me for being so impulsive and I told him that I would be back in time for work. He was not impressed, and I noticed a maliciousness about the way he was talking to me about the Natal trip. I nevertheless crashed in his spare room and when I woke the next morning to get ready for the long drive, I noticed that he had packed a small bag. "I am coming with you" is all he said. I did not argue but contemplated a possible awkward ride with the tall guy, the pianist, myself and the couple, but did not dwell on it for long. I was looking forward to the trip.

When we got downstairs, Christopher, the tall guy, and the couple were already waiting. The pianist got into the driver's seat and said "I think the three of you can sit at the back and you, Madame, will be my co-driver." I did not argue. We loaded the car with the various bags and started for beach on the east coast. There was silence in the car for the first hour and I did not have any need or urge to break the silence.

After a while, Christopher interrupted the uncomfortable silence and asked me,

Madame, do you have a boyfriend?

Absolutely not. What about you, Christopher? Do you have a girlfriend?

Absolutely not.

Good, so you join me here in the backseat when we next stop?

Absolutely, I said with a smile.

When we got to the filling station at Harrismith, I went to sit next to Christopher and the pianist decided to join us on the back seat, because he was tired of driving. Christopher was an imposing character who had an obvious itch for me. He put his arms around me and caressed my forehead, neck and cheeks with kisses. He told me that he hadn't slept the night before in anticipation of this road trip with me. I enjoyed the attention and had no fear or reservations about pursuing this. I did not think about it, I just allowed him to lavish all the attention he desired on me. And it felt good!

When we got to Durban we parked at the Marine Parade and walked around the beachfront. Christopher suggested we find a fish restaurant and we all walked together until we found one. We were all laughing and enjoying the fish and sounds of Durban on New Year's day. The pianist was quiet but I knew that he had a way of getting into his silence at times and left him to his world. After a few hours walking around the Durban beach front we agreed to continue on to Ifafa Beach, which was less than two hours away. We resumed the journey and the man drove, knowing the direction to the beach. When we got there we checked into a chalet. It was a beautiful and rustic type of setting and the ideal place for a getaway from the bustling city streets of Johannesburg. We rested for a while and joined a group of people around a fire near the water, who told us that there was a party scheduled for the next evening, with live music and disk jockeys and that we should join. We later went skinny dipping, feeling like children who had just escaped from a monastery. We all joined in the fun and I do not think anyone felt uncomfortable with the nudity. It was just in the air that anything was fair game.

The chalet was not really designed for five adults. It had a bedroom and the lounge area had a few mattresses. The couple slept in the bedroom and the remaining three of us each found a mattress, and we all quickly fell asleep. The long journey, running around on the beach and skinny dipping had tired us out, and the wine we had been drinking since we arrived there had laid the final blow on our energy levels. We all slept and got up feeling refreshed. We had breakfast at the facilities' dining area and Christopher bought champagne for us to share. We walked around the town and bought some swimming wear and other trinkets from that area. There was not as much tension among us the next day, and I think we all enjoyed spending time together. We found a place with pool tables and spent hours playing pool with other tourists and the locals. By the time we got back to the chalet it was late afternoon and I wanted to nap before the evening activities, which by all accounts would involve much dancing and drinking.

We had a great evening, met many people and we danced in a group with others, by ourselves, and Christopher and I danced together too. After the midnight hour we were still out there dancing and partying hard. I had so much fun. The pianist came to sit next to me at this time and told me that he enjoyed seeing me this happy. We spoke about Ricky at length, who had gone underground with the ANC a few months earlier, and we spoke about how his life and his plans had changed. Christopher soon joined us, put his arms around me and started up a conversation about someone we all knew. We sat there, the three of us talking about everything and anything. There was a nice peace between us.

I slept peacefully that night and woke up feeling at peace and happy. I felt quite close to the pianist and Christopher and enjoyed being there with them. Perhaps the triangle reminded me of Ricky and I realised how much I missed him. When we went to breakfast the next morning, I recognised someone from my past and it changed my mood instantly. The youngest son of that Cruella from Harding was there. I recognised him straight away and he recognised me. He waved greetings at me and as he moved towards our direction, I tightened my grip around Chris' arm and did not let him go.

He told me about how his family was doing and enquired about my life and I told him that Christopher was my fiancé, that I had graduated from university and was working in Johannesburg. He said it was good to see me and I remained silent to that. I introduced him to the pianist and Christopher, and told him that we were going to eat as we had to leave. He said I should go around to his mother's house, who had moved to this area. My stomach turned and I said we were in a hurry and could not go there. He said his mother had told him that I had graduated and I wondered how she knew and why she would be following my life! Really? I clearly recall that her projection for my life was that I would be lost and pregnant by the time I was sixteen. He said he would go up to the house and tell them that I was there and they would come and see me. I just hated it when the different parts of my life came together, forgetting that they had their own spaces in silos where I preferred they remain.

I told the two that I needed to leave that place urgently, and they both sensed that I needed help to escape. The pianist suggested we not eat there, but rather buy food along the way, and in less than ten minutes we had left Ifafa Beach.

Any attempts by Christopher to hug or kiss me after that were met with killer stares and cold rebukes. The journey back home was silent, there were only three of us because the couple decided to stay in Ifafa Beach longer. Christopher and the pianist sat up front and I read a book for the entire journey. Christopher and I were never to share another intimate moment again.

One has to take the risk

I wondered whether that explained why I was still a virgin, probably the only one in my circles and at work. My sexual encounters to that point involved flirting along with people at university, kissing Angeline at the spin the bottle session in Ricky's flat, and kissing three guys. That is as far as it got. Any attempts by anyone to take any sexual activity or romance further than that were met by a shut down from me and a suppression of any feelings or hormone ravings to a place deep down not easily accessible.

I was accustomed to putting other people together and enjoyed playing the matchmaker role. There were many romances that I actively facilitated at boarding school, at university and in our social scene. I was always trying to find romantic partners for Ricky and the pianist as well. There was a girl, Trina, that the pianist would hook up with while on campus and she really was into him, but he was not that keen on her. He often said he was looking for a real woman who was intelligent, and did not wear lots of face paint.

But they did hook up and I always tried to get him to go out with this interesting and intelligent woman I had met through his friend Thabiso. She was bright and I admired her quick wit and her ability to argue. She did not wear makeup and was very organic. Ricky once commented that I was trying to find a version of me for the pianist but I did not believe that was the case. She was free spirited and cared less what other people said about her, and I liked that about her. She had her own rhythm when she danced and always seemed to be having a good time when I would see her. I thought she would be a good match for my pianist friend.

A few weeks after we returned from Durban, it was early evening, we were on his balcony and I suggested we visit this woman and that he should make a move on her. He was silent while I went on and on about why she was right for him and why I thought they were suited to each other. Then he stood up and banged his fists very hard against the wall until there was bruising and some blood on this fist. Then he turned to me, looked into my eyes and said with a loud voice that scared me, "Can you just please stop organising women for me! Just stop it! I am not interested in your theories and your philosophies! Do you think I need help to find women? I can decide for myself who to be with!"

Then he went into the bathroom, probably to dress the bruising on his fists, but was soon back, screaming at the top of his breath, "Hey missy do you really think that I am so pitiful that I cannot arrange a woman for myself? Huh? Answer me! Don't just sit there, and don't you dare start to cry! Today you going to tell me what's going on in that head of yours."

He walked back in the bathroom, and returned to continue his ramblings.

"Come to think of it, why can't you arrange yourself for me? Do you think I enjoyed watching you snog Christopher for two days? Did you ever think about how I felt? So tell me, can you organise yourself for me? Can you? Let's make that your new assignment or new project for me!"

No thought or word crossed my mind or my mouth. I just stood there, looking at him. He was sitting down in the lounge facing the balcony with his head in his broken hands looking down onto the floor in front of him. I did not understand where that came from. The pianist was a gentle soul, never raising his voice, who approached life with a curiosity. I never saw him once angry or upset with anyone. Where did this come from?

I just could not understand it. We stayed that way for a long time. There was complete silence, neither of us moved or said anything after that. Eventually he stood up, walked towards me and said:

"I love you…I need you.

"I have loved you since I met you.

"I have been waiting for you to love me too.

"Please tell me that you love me too…please!"

Before I could answer, he reached out and drew me towards him and began to kiss me. I escaped into my world, I just couldn't deal with this. It was too much. I tried to stay in that world but he was whispering something in my ear and when I tried to tune in to his voice, my own world started to crumble and I could not find my way back to it. I was lost between two worlds, a purgatory of sorts, and the earth beneath my feet I did not feel. I was gasping for air, for I could not breathe, and trying desperately to find footing in some world, any world, but it evaded me. And then I felt what Neil Armstrong must have felt when he landed on the moon, there was no gravity and slowly that desperation to find air and earth gave way to a lightness. A lightness so intense, so free and so full of nothingness and everything, that my consciousness left me. Then I remembered, I had seen the door to this space once before, on an afternoon in a music room. I had shut the door to this space before but now I was walking in that space and there was no world I could call on to help me find my way out of there, least of all shut its door. It came to mind in a second that God must have felt that way when he created.

When I regained any kind of consciousness I was standing in front of the pianist and he was smiling, with tears flowing from his eyes, telling me how long he had waited to kiss my lips and hold me close to him. In all this time that I knew him, I had never seen him cry. He

182

was one of those guys that most women wanted, but he never seemed emotional or available. He took my hand and led me to his room and said we needed to listen to something that he had always dreamt of playing in this moment. We sat on the bed, facing each other and looking into each other's souls, when the sounds of Shirley Bassey joined our state of bliss and awe.

Well I can't forget this evening,
and your face when you were leaving
But I guess that's just the way the story goes,
You always smile but in your eyes the sorry shows,
Yes it shows
No I can't forget tomorrow
when I think about my sorrow
I had you there, then I let you go
Now it's only fair that I should let you go
But you should know...
I can't live, if living is without you,
I can't live, I can't live any more...
I can't live, if living is without you
I can't live, I can't live any more

We never uttered another word that evening, the other tracks followed from the sensuous and binding lips of Shirley, *Till*, *And I Love You So*, *You*...throughout the night.

We fell asleep that night in each other's arms and had a heavenly sanctioned sleep.

I opened my eyes the next morning in March of 1989 to the pianist's eyes fixed on mine. He smiled a smile that had never graced his face before, and his eyes were free and open and radiating pure love. It was a beautiful sight to behold, for they were radiating for me. There was a calm sense over me and an excitement too. We could not stop touching each other and moved between the room, lounge and kitchen as if in a dance. We started to cook something together around mid morning, and kept looking at each other with a smile. Perhaps we were both trying to figure out how we held up such powerful attraction for so long, or perhaps we were just trying to make sure that last night was not a dream. When we realised that we needed items from the store, he asked me to go with him, as if fearful that when he returned the music would have stopped playing. But I assured him I would be fine and that he would find me right here in his place waiting for him. Reluctantly he left. I had the urge to invite Shirley into my space and put at full volume this song with big band sounds that always got me to me feet.

Let me sing a funny song
With crazy words that roll along
And if my song can start you laughing
I'm happy, yes happy

Let me sing a sad refrain
Of broken hearts that loved in vain
And if my song can start you crying
I'm happy, ooh, happy

Let me croon a lowdown blues
to lift you out of your seat
If my song can reach your shoes
And start you tapping your feet
I'm happy

I sang and danced around that apartment in full voice, complete with the dramatic arm gestures of Ms Bassey and when the song would end I would repeat it over and over again. I performed as if the whole world could see how happy I was. The internal happiness needed outward expression and Shirley sure provided the medium. I was so happy that I could not stop dancing and singing all around the lounge. I had not noticed the source of my happiness entering the flat, I was oblivious to all around me. I do not know for how long he was there, and became aware of his presence when I made a typical Shirley twirl movement, imagining I was wearing a long flowing dress; then I noticed him there, watching me with a wide smile on his face. He came to me and held me close and said, "My dear, this is how I have always imagined that love would be." Our emotions were overwhelming and no words could express what it is that our souls had been longing for.

While we were eating he said, "You know you are going to marry me." I had no response to that and he never pushed me for an answer. This man really knew me. He said he had the urge to play the piano, and I wanted to sing. We agreed to go to the university music department that afternoon and luckily we found one of the piano rooms open. He played that piano that day with an intensity and softness and he filled my heart with his sounds. I sat there and watched this man and knew he was moulded and crafted for me. When the music spirit relaxed inside him, he beckoned me to him and said, "We need to start making some music together."

I don't think it would be accurate to describe the weeks after this day as a courtship, but rather a gluing process. We were together almost each waking moment. We went to watch the *Unbearable Lightness of Being* starring Daniel Day Lewis too many times together, we went to jazz clubs together, we made music together, we went to political and trade union led protests and marches together and we sampled almost all the restaurants in Johannesburg together. We fell in love with meze platters at a Greek restaurant, tried

185

sushi, ate prawns and lobster, discovered lots of wine together. We also went for long walks and would spend long afternoons at the Emmerentia Dam and the Zoo Lake. I was happy, he was happy and that was that.

But as you would have it things did come to an abrupt halt in mid April of 1989. One evening, the pianist had said he would come to my place for dinner after he had dropped something off for his mother. He came at least an hour after he said he would be there. When I opened the door and looked at him I knew that I had to ask the question, cause I had sensed something was different. I said:

So are you going to tell me what you were doing?

Don't be angry, but I met with Trina for coffee.

Silence, and I look at him in his eyes.

I met to tell her that she must stop expecting anything from me, and told her that I am with someone that I love very much.

Silence

Please say something I cannot bear for you to be angry with me.

Silence

Please, please say something. You know there is no one but you for me. I had to talk to her because she kept trying to reach me.

Silence

I asked him to leave, and I asked him to stop protesting and begging because it was unbecoming. I told him to pull himself together and just walk through the door and not say another word. I walked calmly and deliberately to my door, opened it and never uttered another word. I stayed at that door for about ten minutes before he got the message and he left. He was muttering many things but by then I had found the world I lost on that night in early March, and in its safety I heard nothing that he said. I was in my own world.

That night, the day after, and many days after that I became very productive and I created a routine to catch up on all the things that I had been neglecting. I woke up in the morning, went to the local gym and worked out for about an hour, came back home, got ready for work, prepared lunch, went to work, worked studiously, had lunch in my office, worked more after lunch until it was time to go home. I got home, cleaned my flat every day and it was spotless. I read books, did some writing on a novel I was working on, watched television, slept off and repeated the pattern every day for many days.

On the second day he came into my office, and asked to speak to me. I took a piece of paper and wrote down, "I do not wish to speak to you. Please do not bother me. I have nothing to say to you. Turn around and leave me be. DO NOT COME TO MY OFFICE AGAIN."

I held up the piece of paper and he read it. Each time he tried to say anything I would look him squarely in the eyes, hold up that piece of paper and I never uttered a word. Eventually he got the message and left.

The next day I found a note under my door. I picked it up and put it on the dresser and went about my business as usual. I would find notes on my car, on the door and each time I would put them aside and go about my business. One day Janine asked me to give her a lift to town. When I got to her flat to fetch her, she gestured for me to come upstairs for a while. When I got there the pianist was there. He tried to speak to me and I turned around, went to my car and drove back to my place.

On another occasion I walked to Janine's apartment, which was just down the road from mine. She had started seeing Thabiso and they made a beautiful and lively couple. I spent about an hour there chatting with them and had a glass of wine. The pianist walked in, greeted everyone and proceeded to have a glass of wine. I ignored him and kept talking to Janine. I could feel him watching me, but did not flinch. He started speaking louder, making many specific references to me. About how cold and uncaring I was, commenting on my way of making people feel like they do not matter. I got up without flinching, bid Janine and Thabiso goodbye and left their flat. While I was walking to my apartment, he came up behind me, and continued his ravings that he had begun in the flat. I stopped, turned around and looked at him. He stopped too, as if afraid to catch up to me. I stared him down, noticed that his beard was growing and that he had a bottle of wine in his hand. I turned around and kept walking. This agitated him no end.

"You are so self righteous, Madame.

"Just take your self-righteous self and go and watch your MNET in you nice apartment.

"Cold, that's what you are! Cold, Cold Heart! Ice running through your veins.

"Thinking that you are better than all of us.

"Nothing touches you, hey!

"No one can come near the ice maiden!

"Ms Self Righteous."

I heard everything he said. I did not walk faster but steadily and deliberately with my head held high. When I got to the gate at the entrance to my building, I unlocked it and went inside, closed the gate and proceeded to lock it again. At this point I was facing him on the other side of the gate. "Are you just going to go in there without a word?" I lifted my head, looked at him and walked to the lifts. I heard him saying "Please, baby, I am sorry for everything I said, I love you, please open for me." But I continued into the lift and went up to my room to allow my righteous self to watch my cable television, MNET, and I enjoyed it…to the fullest!

Later that night, I heard a knock at my door and knew it was him, so I did not answer. He muttered all sorts of insults, threats, apologies, refrains and comebacks but I did not answer him. He stayed there for about an hour and I heard him talk to the neighbours at some point. I ignored it all until he left. I was in my world and unaffected and untouchable.

The following weekend I went to a party at Ricky's brother's house in Bezuidenhout Valley. The party was abuzz with music and dancing. I was not really in the mood for a party but had agreed to drive some of my friends there. I was sitting on the floor in the lounge area with other party goers. I was introduced to some guys who had just arrived from Cape Town. I struck up a neither here nor there conversation with one guy. But he was very funny and was telling stories in weird accents and I started to laugh. Something I had not done in weeks. I laughed until my gut hurt, and I eventually gave in to having a glass of wine with him. He was very funny and was in the middle of telling me a funny story about the place where he came from, when I heard this familiar voice:

"So are you happy laughing and talking with her? Laughing, laughing, laughing, Ha…Ha…Ha…! Trying to get her to laugh at your stupid jokes."

The guy tried to calm him down and reassure him that he was just at a party making friendly conversation with a friendly face. But all attempts to calm him down just infuriated him more. He challenged the guy to meet him outside. I had known this man for some time now, but I did not think that he was capable of this! The guy said, "Bro, I will go outside because I do not believe that a woman like this should be subjected to such disrespect." Of course this escalated the chaos that was unfolding, but men have a way of letting their egos out to play, no matter what the consequence.

They went outside, and I decided it was time to leave. As long as I was there he would not stop. I bid farewell to the host and the friends I had driven to the party and made for the door. The two of them were squaring up outside when I was leaving, and the other guys around them were urging them to stop the madness. I got into my car and drove away. I made sure he saw me drive away, as I knew it would dissipate the tensions and unpleasantness that I was leaving behind.

I went to my apartment, and decided to read a book. I put on some music in the background, but that was a mistake. That music started to break down the walls of the world I was securely residing in. It was a compilation of violin music that he had made for me, and it started to disturb my walls. I was emotionless for those weeks and felt nothing about what was inside me or what the pianist was doing or saying. I was unaffected by the steps he had taken or the conciliatory gestures he had made to try to reconcile with me. By then I had a heap of messages on my dresser that I had not opened and read. But the sounds of those violins started to break down this facade and I was not ready for the flood of emotions that took over me. I started to cry and shake. I considered what he had done to make me that mad. He was not a liar. Lying did not come easily to this Aquarian who saw himself as the bearer of light and truth. He had told me where he was and had not lied, that's got to count for something, has it not? Then I considered all the notes and started reading them; each one of them made me cry except one which read "What's on Mnet tonight?" I simpered to that one. But the others touched me and stirred feelings buried deep within.

The next night I heard a noise at my window and before I could respond I heard his voice asking me to please take him back. Now, I lived on one of the top floors in that apartment building and there were no balconies on that side of the building. This means he climbed on the water pipes from the parking garage level over six floors to reach my window. It was dangerous to say the least. I don't know how he did it to this day. It is very difficult for me to come out from my world, even if cracks are starting to show. I sat on that bed and heard everything he was saying at that window, about how he did not know love until he knew me, about how he was willing to do whatever it takes to make things right, about there being no other woman that lives in his heart accept me. He missed my smile, my kisses and conversations.

It is not that I was not feeling anything, I was, but it is difficult. I just sat there holding one of my soft toys close to me until I heard him going down those pipes. I was grateful that he had survived those water pipes. I thought about things for the rest of the night and decided that he had done enough. I missed him terribly, I missed the friendship, the laughter, the esoteric discussions, the little bumps on the skin of his legs, and his eyebrows. He had these thick eyebrows and slanting eyes that made him a sought after man at campus and everywhere we went. But I loved those eyes and nose and mouth because they all worked together to create a smile that showed me that he loved me. I would wait for the next time he reached out to me, if he knocked at the door, I would open it.

The next day I hoped that he would come knocking at the door, but he did not. I started yearning for him each day. I would walk down the street hoping that he would see me, but over the next few days, nothing. No sound or sight of him. I was going mad but I was too proud to do anything about it. I cried a silent cry for the possibility that he had moved on. Maybe that climb up the water pipes was his last and final attempt in trying to get me back. I was becoming increasingly desperate to see him again and I was falling apart inside. The days and nights were getting longer and longer. It was about seven weeks since we had parted, and since I had spoken a word to him.

I thought about why I had really blocked him out for those weeks and realised that I was so scared of being hurt. Love is a weird thing, you feel so strong and invincible when you are with that person, but you also vulnerable and at that point you are at your weakest. You open up yourself completely to someone and have no protection mechanism in place. When you get a blow or disappointment it hurts to the core of you. I wondered what would happen if I just opened the door to my heart again. But the pain I was feeling now, missing him so much, struggling to breathe; he was like the oxygen I needed to breathe and it was very scary.

I was thinking through all these things when there was a knock at the door. I sat on that bed and could not answer. Then he said "Please open the door, I need to speak to you and see you, I am going mad and I don't know what to do…let's just talk and if you never want to see me again after this, I promise I will stay away." I kept quiet and he said, "I will stay here until you open the door, I am not going anywhere." I was scared of opening up to this man again after realising how much I needed him. I walked to the door and stood there for some time, contemplating my next move. I could feel his energy through that door, it was intense, and he could sense mine too, for he whispered "Come on, open the door." I stood there very confused, and after sometime I got the courage to do something. I unlocked the latch softly and walked back to the bed and sat there wondering if he would figure out that he just had to turn the door knob. I waited and then I heard the door knob turning.

I closed my eyes, with fear and anticipation consuming my entire being. I felt him come closer to me. And he stood there for a few minutes, just looking at me. My eyes were closed but I could feel his eyes penetrating through me like a laser beam. He took my hand into his, said nothing for a while. I opened my eyes and looked at him. I didn't say a word. He laid down next to me "May I hold you, please?" I nodded. He enveloped me and I felt safe, at home, at peace. I closed my eyes and took it all in. Then he started to caress my face with his hands. "I never want us to be apart again. From today can we promise not to spend a single day apart?" I nodded. "You have nothing to worry about or fear, there is only you, no one gets me the way you do. My happiness is tied to you being around and me loving you. The world makes sense when you are around. I belong to you and you to me. Will you marry me?"

I could not speak, I just nodded my head in agreement. What followed was a moment of creation. Our bodies, mind and spirit danced to the quintessential music of life and in that moment we were forever bound. That night our spirits joined forces and soared way above the clouds like mystic eagles and found the meaning of life. Our bodies united at last, allowed mother nature to speak undulating waves of rhythm through movement for which we had no control. We surrendered to her and she had her way with us. Our minds in unison agreed that no thought was required, for it had had its way far too long, it was the time of the universe, of God and the mind agreed to a death.

We were soul mates, of this we had no doubt.

My soul mate, Nesta, approached our decision to marry with an urgency I had never seen from him before. He was excited and determined when he woke me the next morning to tell me his plans. We were to be married before the year was over. He wanted to tell his parents that day and my parents over the following weekend. The parents thing freaked me out just a bit, but I quickly relaxed because he seemed to have a plan, and in it he was going to do all the talking. Eventually we agreed that he would inform his parents that we would come for lunch on that Sunday, and I was to inform my parents that we would visit the following weekend. He was not wasting any time and if he had it his way, we would be married in a month. But I knew that my father would never agree to that.

I phoned my home and my mother answered the phone. I told her that I would be coming home and that I would bring a friend with me. She agreed and gave me a list of things to bring with me from Johannesburg. Nesta called his home and told his mother that he would be coming with me for lunch on Sunday. As the day went along, the nervous energy about going for lunch that Sunday escalated, but he kept reassuring me that I had nothing to worry about.

We arrived at his parents' home and he was smiling from ear to ear. The table was set in the kitchen and the smells from that kitchen were divine. His mother was really good in the kitchen. The food was good and I was enjoying the puris she had made with lamb curry. Then Nesta, who was sitting directly opposite me, started to speak. "I have really good news. This beautiful woman has agreed to marry me. We getting married!" he announced with a broad grin and feeling of pride. Although everyone knew that his mother was a strong and stern woman who no one just messed around with, what followed was unexpected and wiped the grin right off his face. "Don't give me indigestion! Do you want me to throw up all over this table. Why can't you just let us enjoy the food!" I immediately thought of Cruella of Harding, but then I expelled that image from my mind immediately. I could not let her come into this moment and take my joy away from me.

My eyes were fixed on Nesta and no one else. I saw his face change. I examined each and every line of his face as if in a medical examination, and that is where my eyes stayed glued for the remainder of the time at the table. I saw his smile transform into a frown and as if he was talking to himself, the frown was replaced by a calmness. Everything on that face looked peaceful and resolute at the same time. I do not know how long the silence lasted, but he slowly looked up, into my eyes and said with a gentle strength, "This here is my wife, I love her, she makes me happy and I will marry her before the year is over," and then he smiled and kept his gaze into my eyes. Silence followed, but we kept our eyes fixed on each other and I smiled back at him, for in that moment I knew that nothing would change his mind. I also knew that the next weekend would be fine.

There is something that happens to a man who has crossed his own Rubicon for love, he has a *sabi* that there can be no other way. Nothing and no one can change the mind of a man who has crossed that line. I am sure in that moment he remembered all he had been through to get to be with me again and knew that there was no other option for him. We smiled into each other with a sense of knowing. He had stood up for us. I had seen before how sons sometimes have a difficult time standing up to their mothers, especially when it comes to their choice in a woman. I had witnessed my brother, who loved a woman, turn away from her because my mother did not approve, because she was older than him. But here on this day as I looked into his eyes, I knew that this was my man. He *sabi* and I *sabi*! I realised too that I had been putting up hurdles and tests for this man, and he had just passed a significant test on this day. I was dealt the winning hand! I heard Etta James "At Last" in my mind and that song took over my thoughts.

I do not choose to remember much of what happened for the rest of that afternoon. Nothing and no one else mattered. Mothers do have influence over their sons, but they also do know their sons very well. And when Nesta spoke those words, she must have known that there was nothing she could have done to influence him. His father filled the awkward silence with questions to his son about when and where. I do not remember all the questions and all the answers he gave, I was at peace.

There is a steadfast surety when it comes to *sabi*. You do not have the need or desire to verify with anyone else. Nesta never discussed with anyone whether it was a good idea to marry me, he just *sabi*'d that that was the only course of action, and I never had to call girlfriends or family and discuss over long sessions of coffee and tears whether I should say yes. I just knew. I *sabi* and he *sabi*. Later in my life I would tell my friends and nieces that when you know, you know. If you are still asking about it and discussing it with other people, then you should know that it is not for you. If you are begging someone to treat you right, and if you are making excuses for someone, or if someone is not honouring you, your time, your mind, your destiny, then it is not for you. Full stop.

I had previously thought about his mother and how she would react. Nesta was her eldest son and she had a special bond with him. She would regularly call him to take her to many places. I noticed that she saw him as more than a son, probably a male friend. She loved theatre, and she would often book tickets for the two of them to go. She called often and I had made a mental note in my mind, long before we declared our love for each other, that any woman that he chose as a partner would struggle. Nesta was also very bright and did very well at school growing up. He was a gifted child and a top student. When he was in high school he was doing advanced mathematics. He had a sharp brain and his mastery of the piano, violin and guitar attested to a very fine mind. What you do well in at school does not readily translate to what you should be doing with your life. Nesta was born to make music, and this is what he should have enrolled for in university. Not only would he have completed his studies, he would probably have had a doctorate in music at a very young age. I have seen this phenomenon over and over again and sometimes with disastrous consequences, and a waste of so much valuable time.

There were a serious of disappointments that he presented his mother with. The reality that he did not complete university must have been a big blow to her system. This was her bright eyed boy who was going to excel in academia. There was much expectation of him to shine post high school the way that he had excelled in academia up until that point. His parents were both educators and she took educational pursuits and advancements very seriously. The other children in the household knew this too, so the expectation on them was less, although that in itself would present other problems for them. This was not the script that was anticipated for him. Then he had a child outside of wedlock. It must have pained her to see the direction that his life was taking, and now this…Marriage? To someone like me!

I understand now why she felt that way. Some of it was motivated by the stalemate in her own marriage. She and her husband did not share a bedroom and by the time her son wanted to marry me, she had not shared a bedroom with her husband in over fifteen years. They co-existed in that house each resigned to the state of affairs. She got very busy with her job, she enrolled at university and got a Bachelor, Honours and Master's degree in education psychology. She also made elaborate cakes and sewed. She sewed curtains, dresses and shirts and later had a special room for her sewing and studies. She focused her attention on mastering cookery, and no one who ate her food had any reason to complain. She also had a life in her church and was active there. Then there were the weekly visits to her mother's house on Saturdays. Later she would travel all over the world. Like her future daughter-in-law, she got very busy to deal with her circumstances.

His father busied himself with reading. He read many books, and even before Nesta's announcement of our nuptials, he would discuss with Ricky and I the latest book he was reading. He read books about the universe and about self power and would relate his latest understandings of self mastery and the power of the mind. He often told me that I had an enormous capacity for love and forgiveness. I never knew what he meant, but he said he could see it. He hardly left the house except to buy things that his wife needed for her cooking or for the house, and to visit the bottle store. He had a love for whisky, which frustrated her no end. While she coped with the state of her marriage by becoming busy, he turned to pursuing the meaning of life and alcohol.

Over the years I have come to realise that people do the best they can given their circumstances. That we all have some form of pain or internal conflict that we mostly subconsciously structure our behavioural patterns around. Some drink, some become fanatical about religion, some shop too much, some gamble, some smoke, some turn to sex addictions, while others get addicted to the attention on social networking and dating sites, requiring more friends and more dates and more encounters to satisfy that which they can find no rest from. All are driven by the same need to dull or deflect the pain, or to manage the fear or insecurities inside of themselves. I saw this clearly reflected in this home because I had become a master at deflection and dulling over the years.

The following weekend we travelled to my parents' home. It took about five and a half hours to get there. Although there was a sense of fear in facing my father, there was also a sense that Nesta has got this one. We arrived and I introduced my Nesta to my family. We have a very welcoming home and Nesta felt it from the time he arrived. He had no idea what I had come from up until he arrived there. Everything was big, and bigger than he had grown up with. There were big trucks and panel vans, big house and big porch, and when we sat down to eat, there were big dishes and big appetites. My brothers were big and tall. The land was big and the mangos, bananas and papayas grew big. Nesta approached life with an inquisitiveness and saw everything that was new and different as something to discover and study and embrace if need be. So he was open to exploring all of this difference and expansiveness. He fitted right in. He was not intimidated by much, including my father, whom his own family and many others feared and or revered.

We arrived when all of my siblings were at home. My father had a sense that there was something brewing and I was later told that he had called all my brothers and sisters to be home for that weekend. My mother had cooked and we sat around the large round tables on the porch and ate together. The porch alone was as big as Nesta's parents' house. My mother said grace and Nesta attacked that food with a passion. Whilst he was used to good food in his home, there were dishes that he had yet to sample. Our home was rich and traditional, and my father tried to keep us rooted in the cultures and traditions of his family. He tasted the *imbito* first before asking what it was, and I explained that it was a wild spinach, then he tasted the *amathumbu*, which were the intestines of a cow. Although my father was the traditional African in the house, it was my mother who had an attachment and affinity to the indigenous foods of the Nguni people. She mastered the preparation of these traditional dishes and would experiment with them no end. She used peanut and chilli to alter and expand them and many people would come to our home to eat her food. There was also something special about my mother's food and to this day when she cooks, there is just something in it that makes me feel good.

My father did not just view our sitting around those tables at meal times as a place for eating. Those times lasted longer than the average meal times of most homes, because those were the moments in which his family would be together and there was much talking that happened over those dinners. There were hardly ever silent moments. Even when everyone was overcome with the tastes of the food they would verbalise their feelings about the food, even if under their breath. Those tables were meeting points for the family in which the day's events would be discussed, or when we would update each other about the happenings in our lives. During those times my father told many jokes, in his way, always involving stories that would make us simper or laugh.

That meal with Nesta present was no exception. My father told many stories, and Nesta laughed with us at the stories my father was relating. But sometimes he laughed when we simpered, because we knew my father and we knew that some of those stories were a set up for a lesson and trap later, or they related to something we had done in the past.

After the meal, Nesta asked my brothers to show him the trucks and earth moving equipment that my father used to hire out. He spent the next few hours with my brothers exploring the place and discovering everything that was new to him. He was convinced that he could drive them after a short lesson from one of the brothers. But he was much too eager to master that skill and did not realise that it takes time to do so. He got something wrong somewhere and had a not too minor accident with one of the earthmoving equipments. My brother came to the house and told my mother and I what had happened. I panicked and thought of what my father's reaction would be. There was also the main reason for our visit, and this was not a good way to start.

My brother advised that we should not tell my father, and that they would fix the damage before my father would notice. But they were to discover who Nesta was. Later, when he had satisfied his appetite for the big machinery, he came down to the house and sat next to me, telling me in animated detail about all the things he was doing and discovering. I loved seeing this side of him, he was like a kid in a candy store. We were relaxing on the lounge chairs on the porch at the time. My father came out to join us, asked of Nesta's experiences with the trucks. He said, "I am very sorry for the accident that happened." My father's face changed. Nesta then went on to explain to my father in detail what happened and how he thought he got had it wrong and started asking questions about hydraulics and the gear systems. My father stood no chance, and found himself answering questions about how those worked. There was a dialogue there and no one else participated. I went into the kitchen and made tea for everyone.

I laid out the tea and cake on the tables and poured some tea for my father and Nesta. Then Nesta said, "Actually, Sir, we are here to talk to you about something important. May we talk? And if so, when would be a good time for you?" Again my father was taken aback by the gutsiness of this man, and he simpered for the first time since we got there. He looked over to my mother and said, "Mary, this young man is asking to talk to us, what do you say?" My dad always deflected things he was not sure of to my mother, as if to give him a chance to think of the appropriate response. It would also give my mother the first take, and if she got it wrong, or he did not agree with it, he could come with the second and final take. My mother responded, "I think it is a good thing for you to talk to us, we will set up the lounge, and speak after we are done with the tea." My father just nodded.

The next thirty minutes or so preceding this meeting I was surprisingly calm, but I distanced myself from Nesta in that time and sat next to my mother. After some ten minutes my father excused himself, saying something about the restroom, and went into the house. We all knew what would happen next, and without fail, after a few minutes we heard the call from the inside of the house – "Mary!" – and my mother went in. It was his normal practice when he was asked for a meeting or when someone wanted to see him. He needed to know what my mother knew and prepare himself. I can imagine him asking my mother what I had told him and what she thought Nesta wanted to see them about. I could wager some serious money that my mother's response was something like this: "I don't know, dear, let us hear what they have to say. She has said nothing to me. I know what you know. But if I just look at things in my own way, I think that he wants to talk to us about marriage."

This would be her typical response, because she first had to exonerate herself from any complicity in any scheme involving their children, to protect herself, but she would venture to give him an opinion to help prepare him for what lay ahead. That was the game and we all knew it. My father would even give the space for us to be alone with my mother so she could gather intelligence to prepare him later. And even when he asked "What do you know about this?" he knew my mother knew something, but she would always have a precursory disclaimer upfront. The truth is that I did tell my mother that Nesta was here to speak to them about his intention to marry me, and by telling her I knew that she would prepare him. No matter the problems in my parents' affairs, they complemented each other and worked as a team. She also knew what she could tell him, and how she should tell him.

After some time, my mother came outside and we who knew the system knew it meant that my father was ready. She would come out, make random comments about the weather or something trivial and find her way from there to indicate that it was time to face the music, something like "Nesta, I don't know how you going to cope with this heat! It is very hot here, something you guys from Johannesburg are not used to, hey? You should go to the country club for a swim later. But let's rather go inside and talk now, so you can swim before it gets too dark." That was my mother's way.

Nesta, my mother and I went to the lounge and the meeting started. My father started the meeting. "You have asked to speak to my wife and I about something. As I sit here I do not have any idea of the reason for this request. So there is nothing I can say really. What do you say, Mary, can we allow the young man to state his reasons?"

Mother: Yes, we have no idea why you asked to speak to us. I have tried to ask my daughter but she is very secretive. I know you and my daughter are friends from university days, isn't it? You and that chap Ricky.

Father: Ricky? Who is that, Mary?

Mother: It is that chap, if you remember well, we saw him on the day when we went to fetch the Skyline from Joburg! He is the one that brought the spare tyre.

Father: Oh that skinny one, yes I think I recall him. I see, I see! So this young man was also at the university?

Mother: Yes he was.

Father: Oh, did you also do psychology with my daughter?

Nesta: No I did not do psychology, I enrolled for chemical engineering, but I did not complete it.

Father: Why?

Nesta:	Because I got bored with the course and decided it is better to work.

Silence. Nesta had no room to be anything other than who he was.

Mother:	All right Nesta, let us give you a chance to talk.
Father:	No, wait, Mary. So you went to university but you did not finish because you got bored?
Nesta:	Yes, Sir. That is the case.
Father:	I see. I see!

Silence

Mother:	Okay, let's allow him to talk.
Father:	Sure, talk, young man, my wife seems to be in big hurry.

My mother simpers.

Nesta:	Thank you for this opportunity for me to speak with you. I asked to come and see you because I love your daughter and I want to ask your permission to marry her.
Father:	Oh! Oh! Oh! Before you go any further. You see. in my culture and in the tradition of this home, when matters like this one are discussed, the

eldest brother and sister must be present. Mary, can you call them because we cannot discuss such matters without them.

My mother leaves for a few seconds and returns with them.

Father: My children, this young man came to see us. I did not know what he was coming to see us about, but he has just told me that it is about marriage to your sister.

Mother: Yes, that is what he says. Let us ALL allow him to say what is on his mind, please!

Nesta: Thank you for giving me the opportunity to speak. I love your sister and I have asked her to marry me. I am here to ask for permission to marry her.

Brother: Nesta, before we go further we need to ask my sister what she says about this. My sister, has this man asked you to marry him?

Me: Yes, he has.

Brother: Do you love him?

Me: Yes, I do.

Brother: Do you want to marry him?

Me:	Yes, I do.
Mother:	Are you sure that this is the man you want to marry? Marriage is not an easy thing, so you have to be sure. Really I have told you before if I had to do it all over again, I would think very carefully before just jumping into marriage.

My father simpers.

Me:	Yes, I am sure.
Brother:	All right, now that I know that my sister agrees to this, Nesta can you tell us of what you were thinking about? When?
Nesta:	I would love to marry her by the end of the year. Sooner if she will agree.
Father:	Why the hurry? Is there something I need to know? Is she pregnant?
Nesta:	No, she is not pregnant, Sir. I would like to marry her sooner because I want us to start our lives together. I love her.
Father:	I want to ask you again, Nesta. Is my daughter pregnant?
Nesta:	No, Sir, she is not pregnant.
Mother:	So you were thinking of a wedding in December?

Nesta:	Yes, if it is convenient for you, we were thinking about the weekend after Christmas.
Father:	Do your parents know that you plan to marry my daughter?
Nesta:	Yes, they do, I told them last week.
Father:	And what do they feel about this?
Nesta:	They have accepted my decision to marry.
Father:	Do they accept my daughter to be your wife?
Nesta:	They accept that I love your daughter and that I am going to marry her.
Brother:	Nesta, what my father wants to know is whether my sister is acceptable to your parents. Have you introduced her to them and what do they feel about your choice?
Nesta:	My mother was at first shocked when I told her that I want to marry. But I made it clear to her and my father that this is the only wife I will ever have. She is my choice and they will be fine with it.
Father:	In other words, what you are telling us, is that your mother is not very happy.

Nesta:	It's not that she is not happy with your daughter, Sir, it's just that she thinks that it is too soon.
Father:	Oh, if that is the reason, I agree with her. I also feel the two of you are rushing this and I cannot understand why. How long do you know my daughter?
Nesta:	I have known her for more than five years, so I do not believe that I should waste any more time.
Father:	Does your mother know that you have known her all this time?
Nesta:	Yes, she does. She has been visiting my home as a friend for some years.
Mother:	Let me not speak out of turn here, Nesta, but I have a sense that your mother is not happy with your choice? I might be wrong but I am having a feeling about this.
Nesta:	I don't think it is about my choice. Your daughter is beautiful, bright, caring, loving and strong. And she is educated and has a good job. I think these are all the characteristics that my mother would like my wife to have.
Brother:	Okay, I see, so would you say that it is just the normal fears mothers have?

Nesta:	Yes, I think so. But you have nothing to worry about because I will love my wife and no harm will come to her from anyone. I will stand up for her and make sure she is always safe from harm.
Father:	Why did you not come with your parents to see us about this important matter?
Nesta:	I wanted to come alone and speak to you by myself first. I was hoping to come back with them later.
Father:	Okay, very good. It is better that way. We will talk with your parents then.
Mother:	When do you think they will be coming down, Nesta?
Nesta:	I was hoping in the next month.
Mother:	Please let us know in time so we can prepare.
Father:	I want to tell you about my daughter upfront so that you do not come and complain to me later. She is a very lazy person and does not like cooking. She will be telling you to buy Kentucky Fried Chicken every day. What do you say about that?
Nesta:	(With a laugh) That is not how I would describe her, not at all. But we will

cook together, or I will cook if she does not feel like it. And if she likes Kentucky Fried Chicken, we will have to buy it.

Father: Oh, I see. Can you provide for her?

Nesta: I will take care of her and make sure that she wants for nothing. This is my wish and my first desire, but I hope we will together work and build a good life for ourselves.

Father: So you want her to work?

Nesta: Really that is up to her if she wants to work or not, but I doubt someone with a mind like hers will be happy staying at home.

Mother: Truly, me I am quite shocked that my daughter has agreed to marry. She always told us that she never wanted to get married. Are you aware of this?

Nesta: Yes, I am fully aware; she would readily tell Ricky and I that she would never marry. She used to say that often, until I asked her to marry me. She could not say no. She is my soul mate.

The meeting lasted about two hours with everyone asking questions and Nesta was answering all of their questions the only way he knew how, honestly and to the point, and with some humour. At the end of the meeting I could see that my father both liked and admired Nesta for his grit and openness. He gave Nesta his blessings. Nesta was happy.

On the other hand my father was worried about my future mother-in-law and he called me into the bedroom to talk to me about it the following morning. He asked me to relate in detail her reactions to the news of the impending marriage. I told him and my mother and left out none of the details and explained that Nesta had stood up for me. My father told me to tread carefully, and let me promise that they would visit before the marriage date.

It must have been refreshing and sobering for my father to encounter a man like Nesta. He was fearless and knew what he wanted. He stood up for what he thought was right, but he was respectful too. That evening we did not go out to the pools, because I told my mother that Nesta could play the piano. So we spent most of the evening with him doing that. A love affair developed from that day between Nesta and my family. They loved him and my mother thought that he was the perfect man for me.

My mother asked if we could do something together and Nesta started to play *Misty*, a Sarah Vaughn number that we had performed together a few times before.

Look at me…I'm as helpless as a kitten up a tree
Never knowing my right foot from my left
My hand from my glove
I'm too misty and too much in love
I'm just too misty and too much in love…
Walk my way
And a thousand violins begin to play
Or it might be the sound of your heaven
That music I hear
I am too misty and too much in love

I noticed that both my parents were teary eyed during that song. Nesta fitted right into this family set-up. He loved music and so did my family. He never got tired of getting request after request, for he loved to play that piano and was happy that my family appreciated it too. We all went to sleep long after midnight, because our appetite for music was insatiable. As for the songs that he did not know, my mother would readily produce sheet music, which he played without hesitation.

My mother asked him what his favourite song was. He indicated that *How Great Thou Art* was the best song ever written, and then Billy Joel's *Just the Two of Us* was probably his second favourite song. Which he proceeded to sing. And as he was singing I imagined what a wonderful future lay ahead for me with this man as my good friend, life partner and lover.

We had breakfast the next morning around the table on the porch and I noticed how happy everyone was. The talk at the table revolved around the upcoming wedding and my sister and I discussed colour schemes and bridesmaids and all that stuff that never interested me in the least before. There was not much time and my mother was cautioning us about planning ahead. In our customs, the father of the bride pays for the wedding and my father knew he was in for it. We discussed where we might have the wedding, and my mother was clear that we would have it at the country club nearby. I was happy with that. My father did make comments about costs, but I noticed that he seemed pleased that I had found someone willing to marry me.

Growing up, my behaviours and ways often drew comments from him and he said on many occasions that he could not see anyone wanting to marry me. He accused me of sleeping with lecturers to get ahead at university and the number of virginity tests I had to endure made me realise that he thought I was very promiscuous. The reality was very far from what must have been going on in his mind.

Regardless of the past, somehow when I was with Nesta, none of that seemed to matter. And when we were driving away from my parents' home that day I began to see the value of my home. My parents fought, and when I was younger my father was violent to my mother and his children, but there was a sense of family. No matter what the problems were between my parents, they shared a room and we witnessed my father wooing my mother on many occasions, especially after he had done something that my mother did not approve of. There was a way he would speak to her that would bring a smile back to her face, and those times there were always extravagant gifts for her. He also loved to tease her through his many stories, to which my mother responded with simpering. We also travelled a lot as a family and my father believed in family as an institution. The talks around the table at meal times also yielded many memories that make me smile to this day. As we drove away, Nesta commented that he liked my family and could not wait to get back for the next visit. That made me very happy.

The next few weeks we were occupied with making plans for the wedding. Nesta and I did everything together. We found someone who would design my wedding dress and we agreed on the colours of the wedding together. We designed the wedding invitations ourselves and went to describe in detail to the printers what we wanted. Even the shoes that I was to wear were chosen by us together. It was a happy but busy time. One Saturday morning we were driving around looking for the souvenirs and gift packs that we were going to give to the attendees at the wedding. I began to feel sick and Nesta took me back to my flat to rest. We lay in the bed for the rest of the day and I felt somewhat better later that evening. Nesta felt that I was not eating enough because I had reduced my caloric intake quite significantly over the past few weeks. He also felt that I was overdoing it at the gym. I agreed to take it easier. But the next day I started to feel sick again. Nesta took me to a doctor in the same block as my apartment in Hillbrow. What we would hear would shock us both. I was pregnant. Not just pregnant, but four months pregnant. I protested. I had been menstruating each month and I could not be pregnant! The doctor explained that some women continue to menstruate for most of the pregnancy. I did not see that coming and I panicked.

What would I tell my father? I cried so much that day. Nesta and I had agreed to starting a family quite soon, he wanted a boy and a girl, only two kids, and he used to talk about the four of us travelling around the world. But neither of us had anticipated this! We counted back and realised that special day when we agreed to marry was the day we conceived our baby. I called up someone I knew at university and they told me that drinking juniper juice concentrate could help me miscarry. I got some and drank it. The next morning nothing had happened. I was in a state of panic. I was lying in the bed feeling miserable when Nesta spoke to me in a calm and reassuring way.

He indicated that the only reason I was in a panic was because I was scared of what my father would say. He said, "You have me now and you have no reason to fear what your father says or does." He told me we should be celebrating that we would have a child to commemorate that great day when our souls found each other. And he added that he looked forward to seeing a little me running around the place. He always made me feel better. And I had to learn to stop figuring things out by myself because I now had someone who had my back. That I really was not used to doing.

I tried to persuade him not to tell anyone, especially our families, but he would hear nothing of it. He said we had nothing to me ashamed of and we should not hide anything. We travelled to my home the following weekend to tell my parents and all hell broke loose. My father was livid. He called the whole family to a meeting, with me alone. And they let me have it. No one really believed that we did not know I was pregnant when we visited earlier. My father said he always knew I was sleeping around. My brothers asked me stupid questions like "How did this happen?" and my father was disappointed. One brother even asked me if Nesta had forced himself on me. My father told Nesta he was disappointed that Nesta had lied to him. And Nesta said "Sir, with respect you should know that I am not in the habit of lying. I have no reason to lie to anyone. I am sorry that you feel this way and if we have disappointed you, but can we not celebrate that you will have a grandchild?" My father was not impressed with that or any other answer Nesta gave to his questions and muttered and groaned the rest of the weekend, much like on that trip to Cape Town when he was angry about my trip to Lesotho.

I later thought about my family's reaction to the news of my pregnancy. Each one of my brothers were already having sex. My eldest brother had two children out of wedlock and all of them were sexually active. I could not understand why they thought it impossible for me to be pregnant. There were different standards for the males and females in my home. My father would often encourage my brothers to "sharpen their tools", referring to going out with women and sleeping with them. I thought about my father's reaction too. Perhaps in the back of his mind, although he was convinced that I was sleeping around, another part of him hoped that I was not. My father was also a prominent person in the community and our wedding was certainly going to make the newspapers, and he did not need the caption to refer to a pregnant daughter!

Nesta did not care much about everyone's reactions to the pregnancy. He had secured his soul mate, and now there was going to be a child as well. He was on top of the world. When we returned to Johannesburg we went for a scan and found out the sex of the baby. There was talk of the release of Nelson Mandela at the time, and it was likely to coincide with the birth month. We laughed over various names that could capture the significance of that moment but none of Mandela's names were very pretty for our baby girl. On that day we decided to create a name that would capture both our names, given the circumstances of the conception. From that day we called her by that name while she was in-utero. We spoke to her everyday and often Nesta would play the piano for her. The focus moved away from the wedding a bit as he would make elaborate plans to teach her the piano and he hoped she would have a voice like mine so that she could play the piano and sing. Nesta and I were inseparable and we began talking about the three of us, rather than the two of us.

There was less than two months left before the wedding and we readied ourselves for it. By the time my wedding came my father had accepted the situation, but there was still a look of disappointment on his face, and all the photographs will attest to that. At least the ones prior to the music and dancing. By that time, his daughter was married and effectively off his hands, and my father could never resist the lure of music, especially when there was an opportunity to dance.

I had a beautiful wedding and I will always be grateful to my parents for that. The morning was busy with all the usual preparations. My dress was a straight cut style with exquisite lace in the front all the way down to the hem. It had a very long trail with Nesta's initial "N" embroidered on it. My head gear was a simple single-layered pearl band that lay from my forehead all the way to the back hairline and held a simple netted veil in place. The bouquet was made for me by my aunt and it held together white roses with some green leaf detail. When I was ready I stood at the top of our staircase which led down to the lower level facing the front entrance of the house. I felt beautiful in that house, probably for the first time. I descended the staircase slowly and deliberately, taking in every step as a step into a new reality. My father was waiting at the bottom of the staircase; he had an irritated look on his face, but I did see just a small smile on his face. My father's sisters were there too, and they told me I looked beautiful.

My youngest paternal aunt had decorated my father's Mercedes with ribbons and she helped me into the car. I drove with my father to the church, which was twenty minutes away. I did not see Nesta the day of the wedding, as was tradition. When I entered the church, it was so full there was not enough room for everyone inside, so some people were standing outside. As I stepped into the church, everyone rose to the sounds of *Here Comes the Bride*. My bridal party of groomsmen and women and flower girls were already in the front of the church. I walked up to the front with my father at my side. He "gave me over" to Nesta at the foot of the altar and I looked at my husband to be and smiled. We smiled throughout the ceremony. My aunt sang *How Great Thou Art* and Nesta's eyes welled up with tears.

The reception was beautiful at the country club, and was decorated with mostly white and some green. My father and my second brother made speeches and so did Nesta's uncle. In Nesta's speech he spoke of how lucky he was to meet me and promised everyone there that he would take care of me. Bongi and her husband were there with their son, and so were Janine and Thabiso. The food looked good, but I was too taken up by the wedding to eat anything. Nesta and I left the wedding party so that I could change into my second dress. He made love to me before we returned to join the wedding party. We danced until after midnight and retired to bed in the early hours of the morning.

The next morning I woke next to my husband and felt very good about that. I went down to the kitchen and joined the women in the kitchen to make breakfast for a very full house of people. There were probably forty people who slept at my parents' home that day. Everyone was calling me "Mrs" and I did not object. The following day Nesta and I left back to Johannesburg to start our new lives.

Living in love

We found a semi-detached house in Bezuidenhout Valley, one of the residential areas in Johannesburg, and were very excited about moving into a house together as a married couple. We needed a bigger living space to accommodate our baby, who was scheduled to join us two months after our wedding.

We had a month to pack up our respective flats in Hillbrow and there was much excitement in the air. Our own excitement about our new life was dwarfed by the buzz in the country regarding the impending release of Nelson Mandela, who had been in prison for longer than my life time. We spoke with our friends about the irony of our being born in the decade when Mandela was sentenced to life in prison, and our daughter would be born two weeks after his release from prison, into a very different world.

The country looked forward to the unbanning of the African National Congress and the Pan Africanist Congress, and the return of many people who were in exile, including Ricky. I know that many of these heroes of our struggle had a commitment that we could only admire. Nesta and Ricky had long talks about our joining the movement outside the country at the time that Nesta and I had revealed our love to each other. This was something that we all wanted to do but I had the view in 1989 that the work to be done was in the country.

It was almost a certainty that in the next year all parties would be unbanned and I did not see the necessity for us to leave the country. But Nesta began to talk about our leaving every day and I could sense the pressure building up inside him. Before our wedding we agreed that we would reassess the situation after our daughter's birth. I did not worry about that scenario at all because I felt we would not have to do that. And I was right.

Ricky made contact with us before the wedding and made arrangements for a meeting which Nesta attended. He confirmed that even on the other side, in exile, people were getting ready for a return to the country although things were still very much in the balance. It hinged on the negotiations between the government and Mandela inside the country, and the other negotiations spearheaded by Oliver Tambo and Thabo Mbeki in the United Kingdom. When Nesta returned from that meeting he was calmer. I asked him if he had told Ricky about our plans to wed and he said "No, that was not the place to discuss those things." In reality Nesta always felt that he had betrayed his friend, who had wanted us to promise that neither of us would make moves on each other. But there are things that are meant to be, and no one should be stopped from fulfilling their destiny. I understood now why Nesta did not want to make that pledge at that time and why it was difficult for him to tell Ricky that we were together and getting married.

But I knew that Ricky was aware of what was going on. The place that we were to move to in Bezuidenhout Valley was next door to his brother's house. And one afternoon, I got a note from the brother saying that Ricky had passed on his regards. Ricky was to be a sorely missed part of our lives in the next year. He just stayed away. We learnt through a mutual friend that he was staying in Cape Town, but neither of us was contacted by him, and all efforts to contact him were in vain.

In the week that Nelson Mandela was released we had already moved into our house, but we decided to watch the events on television with our friends Janine and Thabiso, who were living together at the time. Thabiso had moved into Janine's place, which was much bigger than his. We alternated between being glued to the television that was broadcasting Mandela's release live from the Victor Verster Prison in Cape Town and going to the balcony to scream with the other people on the street who had long begun street parties. We laughed, screamed and cried together at that historic event. We were happy to see Winnie Mandela at his side walking together into freedom.

I was two weeks from giving birth to my daughter and highly pregnant. Nesta and Janine cautioned me about my over zealousness in celebrating the event, but it was difficult to remain calm. There are moments in history that I have read about in books, but to experience it so close, right before my eyes was an indescribable feeling. By the time Mandela arrived in Cape Town city centre to greet the multitudes that had gathered to hear his voice for the first time in almost three decades, the whole county was hysterical. The television showed footage of gatherings all around the country and the lively celebrations in the streets. When he began to speak, it was difficult for me to reconcile the speeches I had learnt and recited at gatherings at university with this man before my eyes. The last photographs of Nelson Mandela were taken twenty seven years prior to his release and the whole world had been waiting with bated breath to see what he looked like. Twenty seven years is a long time, and the years had taken a toll on him. He had entered that prison as a young, energetic, black-haired man with an air about him that characterised great freedom fighters; and he emerged from that prison as an old man who walked slowly and looked very calm, too calm. I cried when I thought that this man was robbed of the equivalent of my total lifetime. I was happy, but very saddened by this reality. We were all silenced when he began to speak, for none of us had ever heard him speak before. There are few moments that can outshine this one in my memory.

In the days following that historic moment there was a sense of purpose and many of the discussions in the bars, at parties and around dinners and pool tables in the local hangouts revolved around what would happen next, and what the "one man one vote" meant for the country. The excitement and anticipation of seeing other leaders released from prison and returning from exile filled the air.

The world was celebrating Mandela's release and those involved in anti-apartheid campaigns and activities everywhere had cause for celebration. But there was a group of people who were scared. Many white South Africans feared for the future. During this time, and for a while after the elections that were held in 1994, there was a general state of panic. Some built underground shelters and many bought provisions and stockpiled their homes and these shelters with food and various survival kits that they thought they would need for the transition. The *swart gevaar* sentiment (black danger) and the *rooi gevaar* sentiment (red danger) escalated during this time.

The apartheid government, the people who had been voting them in by majority and those people who had a vote and did nothing to stop them, were all united in a policy of white race rule, survival and domination, as well as an abhorrence and fear of communism. These two beliefs or ideologies were the glue that held most white people together in their separate homes, communities and public facilities. And now with the release of Mandela and other "terrorists" like him, the fear for what was to come could be felt and seen. White people made up some twenty per cent of South Africa's population and the numbers of the black population frightened them. With a one man one vote system, there was no escape from black rule, everyone could do the math and this was a sure inevitability. And because white people in South Africa were accustomed to rule that equated domination, violence, torture and human rights abuses, they were really scared for themselves and their future in this country.

But Nesta and I had more immediate issues we had to tend to. Our friends helped us to pack boxes from our two apartments and some brought presents for our new home. We hung curtains, found transport to bring to the house the piano that Nesta's parents had given him, arranged the kitchen and went to look for a crib for our baby. We found a quaint one in one of the antique stores in the nearby area and Nesta began to plan how to make the house more baby friendly. In those days before the birth of our child we cooked together, listened to music, made music together and enjoyed all the joys of being a newly married couple.

By this time, Nesta and I had resigned from our respective jobs in that company where we had been working. We had made a pact when we agreed to marry that we were going to live our lives to the full and do what we loved to do. Nesta began writing music and doing part time work for companies in the IT field. He had already secured quite a few clients who were starting to call on him on a regular basis for work. I got part time jobs at two non-governmental organisations and I liked the freedom that the casual work brought, because we had time to do our music.

The area we moved into was the home of musicians. On the right side of the house was a drummer married to a woman who was working at a non-governmental organisation, and on the left side, a group of musicians who were making waves in the music industry. On the corner was a Chinese shop that sold very affordable meals. This was heaven for us. Every day and every night you would hear music coming from the houses around us. There was an open door policy among the musicians in the houses around us and Nesta began to score music for many of the organic musicians we encountered.

Nesta was reluctant for me to go to work so close to the anticipated birth date, but I wanted to finish an assignment I had initiated at the non-governmental organisation I was working at. On the seventh of March he reluctantly took me to work and about mid-day I started to feel the contractions and I called him to tell him the developments. He fetched the bag we had prepared in advance for this moment and we went to the hospital.

I had never thought much about the labour pains I was to experience, because our lives were very full and busy at the time. I could never have anticipated what was to come, and no one could have prepared me for what I was to experience. I assaulted Nesta a few times as those pains were bearing down on me and any attempts from him to get me to breathe just made me want to punch him in the face, hold his mouth and nose closed until he stopped breathing. The pain is so overwhelming that words like soul mate, love, darling, babe or any other that denote happiness feel like a serrated knife searing all of you. And the worst of it was when he said "just breathe, it will get better." How did he know? Had he been through this before? I was livid! And for once he did not know what to do to make me feel better.

When they finally reeled me into the delivery room, he was not permitted to come with me and I had to face the actual birth process on my own. I was both relieved and scared of that prospect. The ordeal was beyond painful and very hard work – now I understood why it was called "labour". And the moment when my daughter's head came out was a sensation that I cannot to this very day adequately describe. In that moment it feels as if your back and pelvis have been squeezed between a giant vice grip, and when the head breaks through, it is like the vice grip severs that area into millions of pieces. There is no other sensation in life that can compare with the shock and awe of childbirth.

But the moment my daughter came out and I heard her crying as she started to breathe on her own I forgot everything else and started to smile and laugh at the miracle before me. The nurse brought my daughter to me and immediately put her on my breast and instinctively she began to suckle. That sensation too is something you can never explain, it has to be experienced.

I had lost too much blood during the birthing process so I fainted after a while. I woke up the next morning feeling really sick. Nesta was there with his family and I do not remember much after that. I was getting weaker and weaker by the hour. By the third day I was still in hospital and I remember Janine saying "She looks like she is dying" to Nesta. I felt that way but I was too weak to speak. I could see the panic on Nesta's face and it made me scared too; I did feel like I was dying. That day I was taken to the Intensive Care Unit but I have no memory of what happened after that. I later got to learn that the placenta was not removed from my uterus during the birthing process and had begun to poison my system. I spent another week recovering from that ordeal.

When I returned home I had to learn how to take care of our baby girl, but there is an instinctive knowledge that is innate in women who have children. I soon felt comfortable taking care of her. Nesta spent much of his time trying to get our girl to smile at him and he would get frustrated at not succeeding. One morning, he went to do some work at a client's offices and after I had bathed her, I wrapped her up in her blanket and put her on our bed. When I looked at her she was looking into my eyes and then she smiled. I picked her up, held her close to me and ran around the house screaming and crying. I felt something move in my spirit when my daughter's and my eyes locked and she smiled at me. I looked at her again and said "Smile for your Mummy" and she smiled again. I was over the moon.

When Nesta returned, I told him about the smile, but he did not believe me. That was a moment for just me and my daughter and no one can take it away. Years later I would need to evoke that memory to reassure myself that my daughter loved me, no matter what the circumstances.

My mother in law was excited about her granddaughter and made clothes and bought educational toys for her. Nesta and I often visited his parents' home and spent much time there watching tennis on television. She also taught me how to make pies and puris. I enjoyed cooking for my husband and he appreciated any gesture I made. He often looked at me and told me how fortunate he was to have met me. He also built suspended cupboards for the wall to make our home child friendly.

I did not return to work because my husband was taking care of us and I wanted to stay home with my baby. Nesta doted on both of us to no end. He built a sand pit on the outside of our house and our daughter loved playing in the sand. He had also converted the second bedroom into a studio and office, in which he would play and write music and also spend hours developing a software programme that he had planned to sell to an IT company. He used to often talk about what would happened when he sold that programme. The money would take care of us while we made music. He wanted the three of us to travel around the world and make music and the sale of this programme would enable this lifestyle.

Sometimes he got quite frustrated with me because I was enjoying mothering my daughter so much that I would not be as eager as him for the long music practice sessions and he began to make jokes about how he had lost his wife to his daughter. Whenever he made these comments I would remind him of the Lebanese poet whom he loved, Khalil Gibran, and would play the record at full volume for him:

Your children are not your children,
They are the sons and daughters of life's longing for itself,
They come through you but not from you,
And though they are with you, they belong not to you

You may give them your love but not your thoughts.
For they have their own thoughts.
You may house their bodies but not their souls,
For their souls dwell in the house of tomorrow,
Which you cannot visit, not even in your dreams.

You may strive to be like them, but seek not to make them like you.

For life goes not backward nor tarries with yesterday.

You are the bows from which your children as living arrows are sent forth.

The archer sees the mark upon the path of the infinite.

And He bends you with His might that His arrows may go swift and far.

Let your bending in the archer's hands be for happiness;

For even as He loves the arrow that flies,

So He loves the bow that is stable.

He would chase me around the house and pin me down and tickle me, and I would scream and laugh until tears rolled down my eyes and he would not stop until I begged and pleaded for mercy. As if my daughter had heard these words and understood them, she was independent very quickly and did not have much time for being carried in the arms much. She went very fast through her development phases and she was bright. I never argued with Nesta when he said that she had his intelligence. She also had a laugh that came from deep down in her soul and I could swear it was a young woman laughing sometimes. She loved life and had a very boisterous outlook of life. She was very energetic and some people would comment that she was hyperactive. But I knew that she just loved life and was happy. She tired me out on many days, but I was happy that my daughter would grow up knowing that she is loved. I told her too often that she was loved and mostly how beautiful she was. Because I knew what it was to grow up not feeling loved, and never being told that you are beautiful.

This time was the happiest I had been in my life. Nothing could compare, nothing could even come close and there was no basis for comparison. He was the man in the house, he made me feel loved, safe, secure and covered. I knew what rest was, and I felt like a woman. I had time to go for lengthy walks, dress up, cook, bake, sew and care for him and my daughter and this brought me much peace and joy. He was the first man I encountered who not only loved me unconditionally, but liked me. I mean…really liked me.

He liked who I was, how I thought, what I did and even how I spoke. Everything that everyone hated about me, he celebrated. I grew up being asked to be quieter and not to be too forward, but he saw my passionate nature and embraced it. He recognised my ability to look ahead and talk about tomorrow as a prerequisite for what we ought to be doing in that moment. He loved my expansive mind and instead of asking me to silence my thoughts he implored me to share my thoughts with his. He welcomed my inquisitive and curious nature because it was very much like his own. We were both known for "loving our space" and there was an underlying sense that each was free to take personal space when it was required, and even in this I felt a certainty…a knowing that that was all right. The most unusual part of our lives together was that although we both loved being alone, while we were together neither of us yearned for solitude. Instead we were drawn into each other's personal spaces with a force beyond our comprehension. We were inseparable.

We often visited my parents' home because Nesta loved my family. He got along fabulously with my brothers and my father and liked being around the expansiveness. He particularly liked listening to my father's stories around those meal times on the porch. Our visits to my parents' home made me connect with my home differently. I started embracing it and also started to look forward to visiting home. When I went there, I was Nesta's wife first and then a daughter in that home; that changed the dynamics of my home for me.

My parents loved our daughter and when she was about eleven months they asked us to let her visit with them. My father would always comment that my daughter was much like my mother, who ate *inyawu yengulube*. From an early age she loved visiting. She was not a clingy baby and had no fear. She was a free spirit and loved to explore. On that occasion she stayed with my parents for two weeks. When she was returned to us she had been potty trained and was wearing underwear. Nesta and I were both stunned at that development. She also started speaking way before her time and Nesta would often comment that any product of the two of us could not help but be smart. And smart she was. Although my father was a very strict man that many feared, she would breach all his walls by climbing up on his lap and pull at his ears and nose and laugh at him until he laughed with her. My father could not keep a straight face and no matter how he wanted to discipline her, he just could not. She always made him laugh, and the two of them would laugh together and that in turn would make us all laugh. She had a way with him that made him softer.

My daughter was full of life, she laughed from her belly and was eager to learn. She soaked up her surroundings like a hungry sponge. She commanded attention from everyone. I would often say that she was going to be in the performing arts because she soaked up attention and thrived on it. Nesta liked to carry her in his arms, but she was not that keen on being held down and would wiggle her way out from his arms and run around, making sounds and entertaining everyone.

She loved the attention, and the more she performed her gestures, the more attention she got. Sometimes he would put her in the car and drive around with her very proudly. "She is way better than both of us" he would often say. This I *sabi*'d.

We loved the outdoors and many times we would go for long walks together with her in the perambulator. We also bought two bicycles and enjoyed riding them. This was our favourite outdoor activity together. On Saturday mornings we would leave at dawn and cycle to his parents' house or to my brother's place. The rides would take up to four hours to complete. In the afternoons we would ride back with aching calf and thigh muscles. When our daughter turned one year old Nesta decided that it was time for her to join us. He bought a carrier, which he fitted to his bicycle, and the three of us would take long bike rides together. She loved these outings no end.

At university Ricky, Nesta and myself together had taken up canoeing as a hobby, but we had not done this in the past two years. But during this time we decided to start paddling again. We would load our gear on the top of our car and spend some hours on the water. We started packing picnic baskets and after the sessions in the water would stay on the lawns for hours taking in nature. Sometimes Nesta would bring my guitar along and write music.

We were living a life that was full with not much worry and stress. We did not have lots of money but we could afford all that we needed. Nesta was working on his IT programme, none of which I understood, and had scheduled to complete it by December of 1991.

In March of that year when our daughter turned one year old we had a party for her. My mother and younger sister were there and so were Nesta's family and our friends. We had a barbeque that day and he was proud of his daughter. We took lots of photographs of that day as she opened her presents.

In our circle of friends were Janine and Thabiso and Bongi and her husband, and we would visit them as much as they would visit us. In the area where we lived our friends were all the musicians around there, who would often come to our place to eat or to work on a new song with Nesta in the studio. Soon many of them would come over to eat the food that I had cooked.

We were happy. We were doing what we loved doing and life was good. In July 1991 we decided to enrol our daughter into a day care facility that was in our street because I wanted to go back to doing some part time work with the trade union organisation that I had been working with before. Nesta was very excited and proud that our daughter was going to day care and in the first week would take her there himself every day and pick her up as well.

We also decided to get a second car so that I would have my own transportation to work when I started working. One of my father's business acquaintances was selling a car and my father helped negotiate a deal with the man. We went to fetch the car one weekend and drove it back to Johannesburg. We did everything together and since the eve of our wedding day, when we slept in different houses, we had never been apart. Even when Nesta went to consult for a client he would often ask me to drive with him, and sometimes I would go and sit in the car and read a book while he was consulting. We were inseparable. One Sunday when his mother had come to take our daughter to spend a few days with them, Nesta took the mattress from our bed and took it to the lounge. He put on some music and told me to stop what I was doing and lie next to him. We lay on that mattress together and he told me that he was very happy. "I am happy." He said that a few times and we held each other close. We both woke up when one of my brothers was tugging at the mattress laughing. "You two are just for each other in your own world. Look at you, you could have been killed! Sleeping with the doors unlocked!" We had dozed off and had been sleeping for about two hours before my brother came.

My brother asked Nesta to travel with him to my parents' home and they were to return the next day. Nesta agreed and they left that afternoon. They travelled safely and he returned in the afternoon as he had promised. It was our first night away from each other! But when he returned he told me that my father had offered to fix our car, and my brother had come back with him to assist him to take the car for repairs. He would leave that day. I was not very happy about his going again and tried to persuade him and my brother to spend the night. But my brother could not wait until the next day because he had appointments elsewhere. I told Nesta to be careful, I was worried that he was tired and I made him a flask of coffee to ensure that he did not fall asleep on the road whilst driving.

He made jokes and laughed at me for fretting about little things, and said "I have never had an accident in my life, I am not like you that has had so many accidents." He tickled me, chased me around the room and told me to stop worrying. He would be back at seven pm sharp! His laughter subsided and he said, "I am happy, so very happy, I love you!"

The suburb stroll

Let's assume you have never really experienced much in the way of breaks, joy and love in your life; you meet someone who you *sabi* to be your "true north" or your soul mate. If you have experienced this, you will know that life changes before you quite dramatically. You have no more need to pretend, no more need to be what you are not, no anxieties about how you look in the morning and suddenly you love the world because you think it is a really beautiful place to live in. Colours seem brighter and sometimes you could swear you were in the company of angels whose only job is to protect you, love you, make your heart grow and sing simultaneously. All around life is good, Jo!

And then one day you are walking through a leafy suburb taking in all of God's beautiful creations, you hear the birds sing their song, you feel the joyful peculiarities of the cobbled pathway beneath your feet, your mind, body and spirit are experiencing all of this together, your heart wears the biggest smile possible, and in all dimensions you are in perfect agreement that life is a song worth singing. Then suddenly and instantaneously, like a comet falling from the sky, your entire being experiences a different song. In a moment you *sabi* that the song in you is different. You don't know how or why, but you just *sabi*...that life as you have experienced it for two years has changed. You just *sabi*. You stop because you know that this is significant.

The rhythm and pattern of your suburb stroll dances to a different tune as you make your way back home. You hear the music loud and clear, but it tells a different story from a moment ago. You feel the need to sprint home; instead your spirit self holds you back and slows you down because it already knows the cause of the music change and spares you a few more moments before the facts and the feeling of *sabi* align, leaving room for no more speculation. But even spirit cannot slow you down forever. You unlock the door, enter the house and the feeling grows more intense. You expect no one there because you left the place empty when you started the leafy suburb stroll, but you just know that this modest and perfect place you call home will be the site of the revelation.

Morning turns to afternoon, afternoon to dusk and you sit in that chair facing the door, your mortal being anticipating the details of what your spirit already knows. Eventually at seven pm sharp, there is a knock at the door. You rise without fear, without pace, because you know revelation has its own time. You cannot fight it and you feel no need to fight it. You open the door, look in the eyes of the news bearers and then you tell them in a clear and steady way what it is that they have come to tell you. "He is dead, isn't he?"

Epilogue: How Great Thou Art

O Lord my God! when I in awesome wonder,
Consider all the works Thy hand hath made.
I see the stars, I hear the mighty thunder
Thy power throughout the universe displayed.

Then sings my soul, my Saviour God to Thee,
How great Thou art! How great Thou art!
Then sings my soul, my Saviour God, to Thee
How great Thou art! How great Thou art!

When through the woods and forest glades I wander,
And hear the birds sing sweetly in the trees;
When I look down from lofty mountain grandeur,
And hear the brook, and feel the gentle breeze
And when I think that God His Son not sparing,
Sent Him to die – I scarce can take it in,
That on the cross my burden gladly bearing
He bled and died to take away my sin.

When Christ shall come with shout of acclamation,
And take me home – what joy shall fill my heart!
Then shall I bow in humble adoration,
And there proclaim, my God, how great Thou art!

Nesta was right, this is a beautiful song; but I could not remember why I was singing this song to myself. I was surprised at how calm the sea was, there were only a few ripples that I had noticed on that beautiful ocean reflecting the heavens and the white clouds above. As I looked into the sea and its awesome reflection I was not sure whether we were in the clouds and reflecting the sea…or were we at sea reflecting the sky? I called out to Nesta, who was at the helm of the ship.

"Do you see what I see?" I asked.

He looked back at me with so much love in his eyes and smiled that beautiful smile. "Of course I see what you see. It's beautiful, isn't it?"

"I want to be around this beautiful place for ever. Let's promise that we will never leave this place," I said, because I had never seen anything as beautiful as this. My heart was full and I was happy.

"Momma, I am going to help Daddy turn the wheel. May I go?"

"Sure, my angel. Be careful not to slip, it is very slippery over there."

I watched our daughter run in her usual excited manner, ignoring my cautionary reply. When I looked again, I noticed that she was not alone. There were familiar friends with her. I was so pleased to see them. They had been my friends for most of my life and we had travelled on so many journeys together and here they were. I started shouting out to them.

"Luthi! Vena! Evy!…Where have you been? It's so good to see you, and you are all here!"

They looked at me with their large eyes and hurriedly put their fingers on their mouths, showing me that I was to be still. I was surprised by this, they had never asked me to be still before. On these journeys and long chats I often made lots of noises and never was I told to shooo!

Evy came to me, held my face between her two hands and said softly,

"You will startle her, she does not know us, be quiet!"

"Yes, you do know her, she is my baby girl and she will love it here," I said excitedly. "I am sorry that I have not brought her before but she will love you, I know she will."

"Don't you ever be sorry – this is your home...remember! We are happy that she is here. She does not know us...do not startle her...give her some time, she will know us, soon," Evy said with a quiet confidence.

She once again joined the others and I noticed that my baby girl was laughing with Vena, who always made me laugh. Evy turned back to look at me as if to say, "I told you so!" She was always so wise and knowing.

I stayed back there and watched my dear friends play with my lively girl. I was so pleased that she was having fun with them. This was indeed a magical place.

I fell asleep and when I woke up I heard music, someone was singing. I looked around to see who was singing that song. *Then sings my soul....How great thou art*. I looked around but could not see anyone singing.

I called out, "Who is singing?"

Evy came back to me and held my hands in her face once again. "I do not hear any singing," she said.

I protested and told Evy to listen carefully, someone was indeed singing! But when I tried to listen again I could no longer hear the sounds of music.

"Oh it must be coming from the other place, Evy! One day we should visit them and join the choir," I said.

"Sure," Evy said, "but first the sweet girl must rest."

"To die would be an awfully big adventure."
Peter Pan

Afterword

"Sabi"

A term which means "to know". It is used commonly among Nigerians to indicate that something is known, with a certainty, and understood, and that no further explanation is required. In fact, further explanation may hinder the knowing

Do you know what you first remembered about who you are? What was your first thought of the world? What is it that you first knew?

My first memory does not come to me as an event, a moment, or a specific recollection, but rather as a knowing. Yes…a knowing! A *sabi*…as an Igbo friend would smirkingly comment. A knowing that somehow, somewhat, somewhere…you just *sabi*. And from that moment the *sabi* finds home in your being, giving birth to a seed in your mind, your soul, your entire being, and you become a slave to it. It finds roots in your thoughts, bearing its fruit in your decisions, words, actions, fears, heroics, acts of kindness, acts of horror, hallucinations, assumptions, obsessions, addictions, accidents, and even in your skills, your talents, your intuitions and your "natural gifts".

I ruminate whether my hunger for solitude, the struggle with math, my aversion for crowds, the potent allurement of the spoken and written word, or even the undying love for tennis was fruit of this seed. An inevitability brought about by the seed of *sabi*. The bleeding heart, crying inconsolably at the movie *My Sister's Keeper*, the inexplicable soul connection to King Arthur and his Knights of the Round Table, the

240

awe and amazement for JRR Tolkien who created an alternative world so grand in his *Lord of the Rings*, routing for the underdog and unfavoured, Jennifer Hudson over Beyoncé Knowles in the movie *Dreamgirls*; or marvelling and envying the Avatar that can command the forces of nature…How much are these the fruits of *sabi*?

Then of course the obsession with astrology. What is it about astrology that has captivated me the way it has? Is it the quest to understand the why and how of *sabi*? Are the planetary alignments at my birth and those of the people I encounter really as potent and consequential as suggested? Is it an attempt to understand why others have luck and others not? Is it the pursuit of understanding the Almighty being that would create a duality within the soul, and from one soul to the other? Is it the hunt for a plausible reason…one that would explain eventually why some people get dealt the aces and Kings, while others draw the fours and fives?

And on this expedition through numerous astrology texts, countless Google searches, and coffee society discussions on astrological meanings, I have an unlikely exchange with a Chinese woman I encounter on a Sunday afternoon jazz session off Louis Botha Road in Johannesburg. She reflects unashamedly that, for a woman, being born in the year of the snake is not really auspicious. "…mean everything difficult, better for a man, not for woman…this is no good…your life is struggle too much, no? You can have some money luck, but too much personal struggle. I sorry for you." Could that explain it?

I spent significant amounts of time reflecting and pondering this woman's observations and wondered whether my life could really be explained by what appears to be arbitrary formations of planets and their alignments. Suppose I had entered the world sixteen hours later, I would have been born in the year of the horse, which by her accounts would have created more favourable conditions for me and an easier life. I missed it by sixteen hours? In any event the search for meaning on these matters has led me to many readings, research obsessions, visits to astrologists and discussions over countless coffee and dinner tables.

I have had a feeling of being different from the time I understood difference and experienced relativity. Different from what? you may be asking. Different from my family members, different from class mates and different from other women. Indeed the remarks from friends and lovers – "I have never met anyone like you" or "You are different from any other I have met" – these helped solidify the view that the difference was not only felt by myself but also experienced by others. This difference has resulted in many brutal ends to relationships, significant stands on "who I am" and plenty of tear-filled eyes and deep depressive spells followed by vows of not ever doing the friendship or love thing again, until the cycle re-emerges to follow a similar pattern of excitement, euphoria, timelessness, reality, insecurity, pain, outburst and rage, suppression, withdrawal and finally resolution.

I often cogitate whether *different* creates *sabi* or whether it is a consequence of it. One of the many therapists I have visited in my life suggests *different* as a result of placement among siblings, noting that my positioning as middle child, as neither first or last, created a character forming and building process that could only read *different*. So there was no choice in that? Choice…a luxury of those who get to choose their parents and birth placement!

My search leads me down the path of Eastern philosophies that suggest that in *this* cycle of my life I chose not only my parents, but also the placement among my siblings. There was something that I needed to learn or experience as part of my ultimate journey, and that these conditions probably provided the most ideal landscape for my learning and growth.

That makes me muse on where I am in these lifecycles and how many more cycles I still have to go through; and what of the previous ones that would make me choose this set of situations and experiences? What did I do in previous lives that made me want to experience this kind of life? Further on I go to explore past lives through further readings and a regression therapist, whom I visited in my mid thirties, none of which help me to explain this "choice". So I must look at other avenues to answer these questions. Avenues not yet travelled, paths not discovered, but ones that I have vowed to travel in the quest to understand the *sabi*. I ponder at this point whether the questions I am asking are the appropriate ones for the answers I seek to find.

Who is God and what role does he play in all of this? I have ventured into the scripts of various religions outside my own to expand my understanding of God. There are times when I have experienced unbridled love and kindness that let me believe that it can only be God that could inspire such selflessness and pure love. There are moments in the peacefulness and stillness of solitude that have moved me to create some amazing works. In those moments I feel as though I have reached a space inside of me that is connected to the eternal source, and in this space there is no noise, no urgency, no need, no stress. Just peace, understanding and love.

One of my experiences of this phenomenon occurred after I had spent some days in solitude, in which I was moved to write. During this time I had to go to the local store to buy milk, where I encountered someone who had been very mean to me. But when I looked at him, what I experienced was not hurt, pain or anger, and without thinking about it, I smiled at him. He was confused by this gesture and hurried away from where I was. I remember looking towards him as he walked away and sending good wishes to him. In that moment, I knew that it was not the normal me, but something bigger, connected perhaps to something pure in me, that was in control that day. A few days later I received an email from the man offering me what was due to me in the first place. It made me see that this state is transformative, not only for the one who has access to it, but for others who are touched by it.

In this space, when I write all seems normal to me at the time, except that I cannot seem to stop writing, and I am not really aware of space and time. I could start writing at five in the morning and only realise it is well after mid-day when there is a knock at the door. But days later when I return to read what I have written, I am in awe and cannot believe that I have written what I am reading from those pages. These experiences take my breath away.

I have come to know that stillness facilitates access to ideas, revelations and insights that are not easily accessible in the cacophony of doctrine, societal norms and expectations, and particularly religious banter. In the stillness the voice inside is louder, much louder, and cannot be ignored.

In my search for meaning I consider the human condition. If there is a pure space inside of us that can access the eternal source, and give rise to great acts of kindness, create masterpiece artworks, inspire life changing technology, and drive a man to risk his life to save a woman and her baby in a flood, where then does that space exist inside us that gives rise to great acts of horror and pain?

A seventeen year old young girl, Anene Booysens is brutally raped and murdered in South Africa. A woman is gang raped in India and left for dead. A man is lynched because he was born with a black skin. Amudha was eighteen years old when she was tortured, stripped and beaten by upper caste men in her village of Malliampatthi in Tamil Nadu, because her community, the Dalits, celebrated a religious festival without inviting the higher caste Gounders. A child of twelve years old is recruited to kill in the fight for access to power. A grandfather sexually abuses his own grandchild. A young woman, Reeva, in the prime of her life is gunned down by a famous sports icon in this rainbow nation we called South Africa.

I am forced to look at duality again, and ponder whether the source is the same.

Who is actually in control? Sometimes I have had the distinct feeling that we are pawns in a game which I do not understand.

Or is it as many thinkers before and during my time have suggested that *we* create the lives *we* live? That we are programmed by the *sabi*. That the *sabi* is the genetic code of our lives and the determinant of what we have, are and will experience. And that if we in fact change what we *sabi* then we re-programme the *we*, which will start creating a new reality, a new world.

Then I close my eyes, and I imagine a world where I *sabi* and you *sabi* that we are okay, as we are.

How to Contact the Author

www.facebook.com/TheSabiDianeBrown

Email: thesabi@mweb.co.za

Blog: dianebrownauthor.com

www.ingramcontent.com/pod-product-compliance
Lightning Source LLC
Chambersburg PA
CBHW020152090426
42734CB00008B/793